in

REAL ESTATE

VGM Professional Careers Series

CAREERS in
REAL ESTATE

MARK ROWH

VGM Career Books

Chicago   New York   San Francisco   Lisbon   London   Madrid   Mexico City
Milan   New Delhi   San Juan   Seoul   Singapore   Sydney   Toronto

Library of Congress Cataloging-in-Publication Data

Rowh, Mark.
    Careers in real estate / Mark Rowh.
        p.   cm. — (VGM professional careers series)
    Includes bibliographical references.
    ISBN 0-658-00054-3 (paperback)
    1. Real estate business—Vocational guidance—United States.   2. Real estate
agents—United States. I. Title. II. Series.

    HD1375 .R67   2002
    333.33′023′73—dc21   2002016834

2 3 4 5 6 7 8 9 0 DOC/DOC 1 0 9 8 7 6 5 4 3

ISBN 0-658-00054-3

McGraw-Hill books are available at special quantity discounts to use as premiums and sales promotions, or for use in corporate training programs. For more information, please write to the Director of Special Sales, Professional Publishing, McGraw-Hill, Two Penn Plaza, New York, NY 10121-2298. Or contact your local bookstore.

This book is printed on acid-free paper.

This book is dedicated to Johnny and Patty Turner.

CONTENTS

CHAPTER 9

Real Estate Counseling and Research   93

The Nature of the Work • The People with Whom Real Estate
Counselors Work • The Settings in Which Real Estate
Counselors Work • Training and Other Qualifications •
Advancement Possibilities • Additional Sources of Information

CHAPTER 10

Real Estate Law   99

The Nature of the Work • The People with Whom Real Estate
Lawyers Work • The Settings in Which Real Estate Lawyers
Work • Training and Other Qualifications • Advancement
Possibilities • Additional Sources of Information

CHAPTER 11

Mortgage Loan Processing   105

The Nature of the Work • The People with Whom Loan Officers
Work • The Settings in Which Loan Officers Work • Training
and Other Qualifications • Advancement Possibilities •
Additional Source of Information

CHAPTER 12

Construction and Building Inspection   113

The Nature of the Work • The People with Whom Building and
Construction Inspectors Work • The Settings in Which Building
and Construction Inspectors Work • Training and Other
Qualifications • Advancement Possibilities • Additional Sources
of Information

CHAPTER 13

Other Jobs Related to Real Estate   119

Title Examiners and Researchers • Real Estate Clerks and
Secretaries • Architects • Insurance Sales Agents • Real Estate
Specialty Positions • Other Related Jobs

ACKNOWLEDGMENTS

The author offers grateful thanks to the following for their cooperation in providing information for this book:

American Society of Farm Managers and Rural Appraisers
Association of Real Estate License Law Officials
Gloria Bowman
Building Owners and Managers Association
Canadian Real Estate Association
Community Associations Institute
The Counselors of Real Estate
Institute of Real Estate Management
National Association of Industrial and Office Properties
Urban Land Institute
U.S. Department of Housing and Urban Development
U.S. Department of Labor
Sheila K. Vertino

Note: Some material has been reproduced courtesy of the Counselors of Real Estate, the Canadian Real Estate Association, and the National Association of Industrial and Office Properties.

C H A P T E R

1

REAL ESTATE OCCUPATIONS

The right to own property is seen by many as basic to our civilization. From private homes or family farms to shopping malls or chemical plants, people own and use property for a variety of purposes.

The amount of property available, however, is finite. When people desire real estate, they must purchase it from others. This process, which can be quite complicated, is bound by a variety of laws and regulations. In most cases, the parties involved need professional assistance to complete the necessary transactions. To support this need, a variety of occupations have emerged over the years.

HISTORY OF REAL ESTATE

Land ownership is virtually as old as civilization itself. In ancient times the concept of ownership was vastly simpler than it is today, with land "belonging" to those who lived on it, but with no formal ownership status, and transfer of property being a haphazard process based on factors as diverse as gifts, illness, or brute force. As civilization progressed, various standards of property ownership developed. In many nations, the concept emerged that most or all property belonged to the king or other leader, or to a select few.

In about the year 3000 B.C., according to the Canadian Real Estate Association, the king of Babylon mandated that for a real estate contract to be legal, it had to be entered into freely by both parties involved. In 2100 B.C. mortgage terms were spelled out on clay tablets, and records of Egyptian property taxes go back as far as 2000 B.C.

During Roman times, the customary interest rate for loans was 1 percent, but only half that amount for mortgages. To advertise real estate holdings, both the ancient Greeks and Romans used criers in public places such as a marketplace or town square. Instead of placing signs on lawns, they often painted an ad directly on the wall of a building for sale.

In later centuries, the right to own property became more common, and increasing numbers of rules and laws were developed governing real estate transactions.

In medieval Europe, the nobility owned most of the land, with the vast majority of people not even eligible to own real estate. But as the centuries passed, a middle class emerged and the concept of individual rights gained increasing strength. As a part of these developments, both the right to buy property and the economic wherewithal to take such a step became more common.

As North America was colonized by European nations, their concepts regarding land ownership became the basis for American laws and practices. Of course there were the unique situations involved in settling a "new" continent whose natives tended to be nomadic or relatively small in population, including measures such as giving land away to settlers. But as the country became more densely populated and time passed, land ownership became more standardized.

Today, a variety of occupations exist that revolve around buying, selling, maintaining, or improving real estate. Men and women working in these career areas provide vital services in helping individuals, families, businesses, government agencies, and nonprofit organizations take real estate–related actions.

In the last one hundred years, home ownership has become more and more common. According to the U.S. Bureau of the Census, almost two-thirds of American households now own their own homes. This is a major change from the start of the twentieth century, when a majority of families did not own the homes in which they lived. Home ownership increased substantially through the 1920s, but then the Great Depression caused a reversal in the fortunes of many, and the home ownership rate fell to 43 percent, its lowest level of the century.

After World War II, several factors worked to make things more favorable for the prospect of home ownership. Economic growth, easier financing, legislation promoting the purchase of homes, and growth in the home construction industry all contributed to improved prospects for American families to buy homes. This in turn fueled the growth of the real estate industry, which has become a major part of the modern business scene.

Another factor increasing the demand for real estate professionals is the growing trend toward moving. Renters have historically moved frequently, but home owners are also surprisingly frequent movers. This includes both those who select newer or larger homes in their own communities, and persons relocating to other cities or states due to job changes or other factors. According to the U.S. Census, over thirty million families or households have moved within the past fifteen months. This common practice means that homes are constantly "turning over," contributing to the continued demand for the assistance of agents, brokers, and other professionals in the field of real estate.

In addition to property used for residential purposes, business growth has resulted in continued demand for business properties. New and expanding businesses are constantly buying new properties, constructing new buildings or other structures, developing underutilized land, and making other changes in which real estate plays a key role.

DEMAND FOR REAL ESTATE PROFESSIONALS

According to the Ohio State University, more than five million people in the United States are employed in real estate or related fields, and more than one-third of the world's wealth is tied up in real estate.

Real estate sales agents alone hold more than 330,000 jobs, according to the U.S. Department of Labor, and real estate brokers have at least 90,000 jobs. Add to those career areas positions such as appraisers, building and construction inspectors, real estate lawyers, property managers, mortgage loan officers, and others, and the dimension of the real estate industry becomes more apparent.

In many ways, real estate is a highly competitive field, and not everyone is successful. Beginning agents, for example, may find it difficult to obtain a sufficient number of listings or to close enough sales. But for those with the right training and the necessary skills, this career area can be a truly rewarding one.

Future Prospects

Looking to the future, a strong demand for real estate professionals is likely to continue. As in the past, ownership of property will be a central element of society, and property will always be changing hands. As the need continues for families to buy and sell homes, and for businesses to purchase, lease, or sell property, the concurrent demand for professional assistance will exist.

On one level, this means that from a pragmatic viewpoint, those making career plans might find that real estate has much to offer. But the benefits of real estate careers even go beyond the potential to provide excellent incomes and a variety of career challenges. It may sound like hyperbole, but one of the greatest pluses of a career in real estate is that in many cases, you can play a role in helping people fulfill their dreams. Whether this means buying a home, opening a small business, or expanding into a larger business facility, buying real estate is often much more than just a financial transaction. In many cases, it is the culmination of years of planning.

Skills Needed

In addition to the specialized knowledge of the field gained through education and experience, real estate professionals need certain skills. Of course these vary within specialty areas and from situation to situation, but in general they include some combination of communication skills, organizational ability, and personal aggressiveness. According to the Ohio State University, persons employed in real estate need a high level of people skills, a very high level of sales skills, and a high level of communication skills.

Do You Have the Right Traits for This Field?

Do you have the traits needed for success as a real estate professional? Consider what the National Association of Industrial and Office Properties says about this matter:

Real estate professionals must be able to research, analyze, negotiate, plan and market. They often work long days. Before discussing skills and career paths, first think about this question: "What am I good at?" An honest self-assessment is a good place to begin before thinking about any career. Imagine a straight line axis with two extreme personality attributes at opposite ends: "analytical" versus "people-oriented." Few of us can ever be both highly analytical and highly people-oriented. Instead, we fall somewhere in between. Analytical types are comfortable with research and analysis, enjoy learning new technical skills, and problem modeling and solving. People-oriented types are extroverts by nature and prefer working with people rather than sitting behind a desk.

Certain real estate specializations tend to require more of the analytical attribute, while others require more of the people-oriented attribute. For example, appraisers, mortgage lenders, corporate real estate managers and property managers must be strong on the analytical side, with strong writing skills. Brokers and leasing agents require strong interpersonal, negotiation and verbal skills. Developers, commercial mortgage brokers, and real estate consultants need a heavy dose of both. Which are you?

Real estate people can never know too much. They must constantly strive to stay abreast of business trends and think about issues—tax laws, new highway routes, technology, or existing and proposed zoning regulations—affecting their clients, business, and investments. Above all, successful real estate professionals are entrepreneurial by nature and process-oriented. They generally look for opportunities and ways to improve business. Real estate entrepreneurs are successful in most business fields and often diversify into other (non–real estate) businesses.

Beyond a general knowledge of business, economics, and a global market perspective, employers expect neophyte real estate professionals to be computer literate, using spreadsheets, database analysis, word processing, graphical analysis, and geographic information systems. They also expect new employees to communicate well and to make oral presentations. Negotiation skills are also an important aspect of the real estate industry, and students should practice these while in school.

The following chapters explore various career paths within the real estate field, describing the nature of the work, the people and settings workers are likely to encounter, and preparation for each type of work, as well as providing many sources of further information.

C H A P T E R

RESIDENTIAL AGENTS AND BROKERS

Real estate agents and brokers serve as the first point of contact when potential home buyers express interest in purchasing a home. It is their role to provide information and advice on various aspects of the home-buying process, as well as information about specific homes that are available. In many cases, brokers and agents serve the interests of the seller rather than those of the buyer. Typically, they are hired by the seller to identify someone who is interested in buying the home in accordance with the desired price and other conditions established by the property's seller.

In some cases, agents and brokers represent the buyer rather than the seller. In this role, they may be known as buyers' brokers. Sometimes the same agent or broker may represent both the buyer and seller in the same transaction, although this is not allowed in all states.

The prices paid for houses are substantial. For many families, purchasing a home is the biggest investment they will ever make. Thus for residential real estate agents and brokers, who earn commissions based on a percentage of a home's sale price, earnings potential can be outstanding. An agent who sells a large number of homes can earn well above the average salary paid to workers in other fields.

Table 2.1 shows a summary of new home prices paid in the United States in recent years, as reported by the U.S. Census Bureau. The median price is the figure for which half of the houses sold below that amount, and half sold above. The average is the numerical average for all homes sold during the time period.

Table 2.1 New Home Prices in the United States

Year	Median	Average
2000	$169,000	$207,000
1999	$161,000	$195,600
1998	$152,500	$181,900
1997	$146,000	$176,200
1996	$140,000	$166,400
1995	$133,900	$158,700
1994	$130,000	$154,500
1993	$126,500	$147,700
1992	$121,500	$144,100
1991	$120,000	$147,200
1990	$122,900	$149,800
1989	$120,000	$148,800
1988	$112,500	$138,300
1987	$104,500	$127,200
1986	$92,000	$111,900
1985	$84,300	$100,800
1984	$79,900	$97,600
1983	$75,300	$89,800
1982	$69,300	$83,900
1981	$68,900	$83,000
1980	$64,600	$76,400

Of course, home prices vary widely according to geographic area. According to the National Association of Home Builders, one of the nation's most affordable housing markets is Kokomo, Indiana, with a median home sale price of $99,000 in 2001. Among larger cities, Kansas City, Missouri, had a median sale price of $130,000 during the same time period. But at the upper extreme, the median price for a house sold in San Francisco was $530,000.

THE NATURE OF THE WORK

The majority of real estate agents and brokers sell single-family homes or other residential properties. Others focus on agricultural, commercial, industrial, or other types of real estate, most typically as employees in large or specialized companies (see later chapters).

Agents Versus Brokers

Real estate agents and brokers perform similar work, and sometimes people outside the field tend to use these terms interchangeably. But there are important distinctions between the two roles. Normally, an agent is a sales worker who works under contract to a licensed real estate broker. When a sale is made the broker receives a commission, and then pays a preset portion to the agent.

In general, the job of a broker is more complex than that of an agent. Brokers function as independent businesspeople. Generally, their primary function is selling real estate owned by others. In the process of selling real estate, brokers take care of various types of background work. Along with taking care of tasks ranging from arranging for title searches to helping buyers obtain financing, they supervise agents who may fulfill many of the same roles. In addition, brokers may also advertise properties for sale, manage their own offices, and take care of other business responsibilities. They may also rent and manage properties. Some brokers combine other types of work with their real estate business. For example, they might practice law, sell insurance, or offer investment products.

Note: Professional realtors and their associations often use the term *REALTOR* (in all uppercase letters) as a copyrighted designation for their profession. For consistency in this book, however, the more generic term *realtor* will be used.

Tasks Performed

While obviously the main goal of agents and brokers is making property sales, this is not a simple or one-dimensional process. As an important preliminary step, they must garner agreements with owners to place properties for sale with their company. Commonly known as obtaining listings, this effort often consumes an appreciable amount of time and energy. Once an agreement to list a property has been made, agents and brokers determine its competitive market price, primarily by comparing it with similar properties that have recently sold. After a property is sold, a portion of the commission is paid to the agent who sold the property, and a share is also paid to the agent who obtained the listing in the first place. Thus the most desirable situation is for an agent to both list and sell the same property.

A common task undertaken by real estate professionals is showing houses or other residential properties to potential buyers. This is often preceded by meetings with buyers during which basic factors are discussed such as how much clients can afford to spend and features they desire in a home. At the same time, a loyalty contract may be signed in which the buyers agree that this agent will be the only one to show them houses.

During these early discussions, real estate professionals may provide information about available properties. This may include photos, printed lists, brochures, or computer-generated information. With the latter, special software may be used to provide clients with a "virtual" tour of any number of houses before an actual visit is made.

Once clients decide they would like to purchase a given property, negotiations may take place in which offers and counteroffers are made. During this bargaining process, the agent may play an important part in communicating information between buyers and sellers.

When an agreement has been reached, the parties involved enter into a written contract. The broker or agent then helps make sure that all provisions of this agreement are carried out before the closing date, the date when the transaction becomes final and the property changes hands. While many details may be handled by lawyers, loan officers, or others, real estate professionals often play a coordinating role in this process.

The actual tasks undertaken by brokers and agents vary from one firm to another as well as among different transactions. In some cases, they may help buyers obtain a mortgage loan. They may also make recommendations about banks or other lenders, attorneys who facilitate real estate transactions, title companies, closing agents, or other aspects of the purchasing process. Clients are not required to follow the real estate broker's recommendations. They may compare the costs and services offered by other providers with those recommended by the real estate broker.

Agents and brokers develop agreements of sale, review them with the parties involved, and make changes or additions agreed to by the buyer and seller. They may help sellers establish the sale price and negotiate changes in this amount, and assist in establishing exactly what (if any) appliances or other personal property will be included with the sale. They may also provide advice in areas such as provisions to be followed if a proposed buyer is unable to gain approval for a loan, inspections regarding the presence of pests or damages from termites or other pests; environmental concerns such as asbestos, radon, or hazardous lead-based paint; and overall home inspections. The latter may cover matters such as the external structural conditions; water drainage on the property; and the condition of plumbing, heating, cooling, and electrical systems. Real estate professionals may also advise their clients on matters such as settlement costs or determining which parties in a transaction are responsible for expenses such as taxes, water and sewer charges, or utility bills at the date of settlement.

Providing Key Information

A primary function for agents is providing information that will help clients reach their own objectives related to buying or selling houses. For example, while agents and brokers do not make loans, the more knowledgeable they are about various loan alternatives, the better prepared they are to deal effectively with potential home buyers.

For example, an agent might inform clients about the options provided by banks, credit unions, savings associations, mortgage companies, and mortgage brokers. He or she might also provide information about government-sponsored loans such as those insured through the Federal Housing Administration or guaranteed by the Department of Veterans Affairs.

Agents and brokers might also be familiar with various types of loans such as fixed-rate loans, in which the principal and interest payments remain the same during the loan term, and several types of variable-rate loans, which can have different indexes and margins that determine how and when the rates and payment amounts change. And by staying on top of trends in interest-rate changes, they can anticipate increases or decreases in the demand for new homes.

It is also helpful for real estate professionals to be familiar with lender-required settlement services and costs. These might include surveys, mortgage insurance, title insurance, appraisals, credit reports, or fees for document preparation, loan processing, flood certification, or underwriting.

The more they know about their clients and the particular needs of potential buyers, the more effective agents and brokers may be. In considering such needs, they may address factors such as whether the space is sufficient for the present and future needs of potential buyers; if there are enough bedrooms and bathrooms; the structural soundness of a house; whether there is a yard and, if so, if its size and configuration are adequate; and whether appliances or structural components should be repaired or replaced. Real estate professionals are also well advised to know details about the neighborhood in which a house is located, including information about nearby schools or churches, the ages of other families (for example, whether any young children live nearby), trends regarding crime or overall safety, and other details. They can use such information in answering questions or providing overviews of the advantages of any given property.

A major part of the job is describing the various features of properties to make them sound as attractive as possible to potential buyers. For example, for a large house situated in a suburban area, an agent might point out that it is built on an eight-acre wooded site featuring a small, beautiful stream, and then focus on the house's structural and internal features. In this case, the agent might point out that this two-story house includes a large deck, four roomy bedrooms, a family room with a fireplace, two full bathrooms and one half-bath, and an efficient heat-pump heating and cooling system. By mastering such information and then conveying it to potential buyers, agents and brokers increase their chances of sales success.

Brokers and agents are also well advised to have a general understanding of real estate financing and related topics. Even though loan officers or other financial professionals may hold primary responsibility for such matters, sales professionals must be able to converse about such details when called upon.

For instance, agents and brokers should be familiar with different types of mortgages such as thirty-year fixed mortgages, fifteen-year fixed mortgages, and one year adjustable rate mortgages. They should also be able to make estimates of monthly payments, down payments, and other details of prospective real estate purchases. Even if they are not directly involved in any aspect of financing, this is useful in helping prospective buyers select potential properties.

For instance, consider a conversation between Timothy, a real estate agent, and the Carrs, a young couple who have not previously owned a home. The Carrs are just beginning the process of looking at a possible house purchase, and they have not yet discussed the matter with a loan officer. While he could defer discussion of finances and focus purely on features of homes listed by his firm, Timothy wants to be as helpful as possible. So he takes a house listing for $110,000 and, using it as an example, discusses with the Carrs some basic financial considerations. He points out that if they make a down payment of $10,000, the Carrs will be financing approximately $100,000. If they take out a thirty-year conventional mortgage at 6.875 percent interest with no points (see discussion of points in the Glossary), their monthly payment will be about $657.

Using a computer, calculator, or chart (or sometimes simply figures committed to memory), he can make similar estimates for other loan amounts or different types of financing. He might also make use of an income estimator to advise the couple on what might be an affordable price range for them to consider. After determining their annual income, he might provide them an estimate of the maximum price they could readily afford for a home.

Negotiating and Conducting Settlements

Another important part of the broker's job is negotiation. Usually, a real estate transaction is more involved than simply having a buyer agree to an initially offered sale price. In the typical case where the agent works for the seller, it is part of the agent's job to keep the sale price as high as possible, while the buyer naturally would like to lower the purchase price, and normally makes an offer that is less than the "asking" price. And of course as high a price as possible is in the agent's best interest, since the higher the sale price, the greater the commission. The agent realizes that a number of factors can be considered in this process, including the age and condition of the home, prices being paid for other homes in the same area, length of time the property has been on the market, and other factors. Taking such matters into consideration, the agent may conduct or assist the seller in a give-and-take negotiation process until both parties agree on a sale price.

The final major step in selling a home is the settlement, where documents are signed and the necessary legal arrangements are finalized. In some cases, settlements are conducted by real estate brokers. In others, they may be conducted by attorneys, lenders, title insurance companies, or escrow companies. Most typically, this process involves a face-to-face meeting by the involved parties or their representatives. An alternative practiced in some states is to place this responsibility with an escrow agent, who gathers the necessary documents and handles the various logistics of the settlement.

Earning Commissions

Commissions are payments made as a percentage of a property's sale price. Usually they are paid to the broker by the seller. Although commission rates vary, a typical percentage is 6 or 7 percent of the cost of a house or other property. At a rate of 6 percent, the commission on a house selling for $150,000 would be $9,000. Obviously this is a significant amount, and the potential to earn large commissions is one of the main attractions of the real estate profession. At the same time, it is important to realize that commissions must often be shared (for example, between a broker and an agent, or between the professional who listed a house and another who actually sold it), and that there is no guarantee than any given number of houses will be sold within a specific time period. Thus the potential earnings that might be realized can vary widely.

Representing Various Types of Properties

The most common type of property bought and sold in the residential area is the private, single-family home used as a primary residence. But agents and brokers may also deal with other types of residential properties.

For instance, a lucrative field in some areas is the sale of vacation properties. Homes used for seasonal, recreational, or occasional use make up a class of properties that offer potential for real estate sales professionals. Beach houses, warm-weather winter getaways, time-sharing condos, and hunting cabins are just some of the examples in this area.

THE PEOPLE WITH WHOM REAL ESTATE AGENTS AND BROKERS WORK

One of the pluses of working in real estate is the chance to work with a variety of people. Serving as a broker or agent can bring in a healthy income, but to be a truly enjoyable occupation, it should provide more in the way of job satisfaction than just financial rewards. Agents and brokers should also gain satisfaction from working with people and helping them reach their goals for housing, business facilities, or other purposes. Fortunately, such opportunities abound. The nature of the real estate profession involves interacting with a diverse array of people.

A real estate agent who specializes in residential sales, for instance, deals with a wide range of clients. In any given week, this might consist of dozens of different people. In one case, a young couple with limited resources might be buying their first house. In another, a large family might be planning to move out of an existing house that is very nice, but is simply too small for their needs. Agents might represent sellers who are young or old, affluent or financially challenged, experienced or inexperienced in dealing with real estate transactions. Clients might be native-born Americans or Canadians, or immigrants from other nations. They might be males, females, couples, or families. They might come from any occupational area and might represent diverse religious, racial, or ethnic backgrounds.

Along with diversity in clients, agents and brokers work with professionals and office workers from a variety of related professions. They routinely interact with bank officials, attorneys, insurance representatives, appraisers, home inspectors, and others. In many communities they play highly visible roles, serving in organizations such as the chamber of commerce or local civic clubs.

THE SETTINGS IN WHICH AGENTS AND BROKERS WORK

Some real estate agents and brokers work in offices, which usually provide comfortable working conditions. These settings range widely in size and configuration, from small offices to larger complexes. Within these settings, most workers enjoy comfortable office furniture, good lighting, temperature controls, and access to computers and other equipment.

Some agents and brokers work primarily out of their homes instead of traditional offices. The growth of the Internet, increased use of E-mail, and other advances in telecommunications have made it practical to use private homes as a base of operations for conducting real estate business. This can be convenient for a number of reasons, from reducing office expenses and gaining tax advantages to increasing time spent with children or other family members.

Whether they work out of an office building or are based in their homes, however, most real estate professionals also spend a great deal of time away from their desk. They are often in the field looking at potential sale properties, showing houses or other properties to customers, meeting with prospective clients, engaging in marketing or community service activities, or completing other tasks. In fact, many agents would tell you their real office is their automobile, since they spend so many hours driving from one site to another.

Quite often, the workweek for agents and brokers exceeds the common standard of forty hours. According to the U.S. Department of Labor, nearly one out of every four works at least fifty hours a week. Regardless of total hours worked, evening and weekend work is usually required, since many customers are unavailable at other times due to their own employment commitments. In addition, real estate professionals are always "on call" and must be responsive to phone calls, requests to look at properties, or other needs expressed by clients. At the same time, the need to work long or irregular hours is balanced by flexibility in setting daily work schedules, taking days off, planning vacations, or meeting other personal needs.

In many parts of the United States and Canada, business tends to be slower during the winter months than in warmer seasons. But this varies by location and can be affected by other factors.

According to the U.S. Department of Labor, more than two-thirds of brokers and agents are self-employed. Many work on a part-time basis, often combining their real estate work with other occupations. While real estate is sold in all geographic areas, employment prospects tend to be greater in heavily populated urban areas or rapidly growing suburban communities.

The majority of real estate firms are small, and some are one-person operations. At the other extreme, some large real estate companies have hundred of agents who operate out of a network of branch offices. In many cases, brokers enter into franchise agreements with regional or national real estate companies, under which the broker pays a fee in order to be able to use the name of the more widely known parent firm.

To get started in this field, one approach is to start out with a large real estate firm that employs a number of agents. Under this approach, agents use such a job to gain experience, and in the process develop options for the future that might include staying with the firm and becoming one of its long-term employees, starting their own firm after gaining experience, or following another path.

While duties may vary from one company to another, typically they might include some combination of providing overall assistance in home buying and selling, attracting clients, showing properties, fostering customer satisfaction, and closing transactions.

TRAINING AND OTHER QUALIFICATIONS

One advantage of this field is that an advanced education is not always necessary. While a college degree can be helpful, many real estate agents have been successful without holding such a degree. As long as they can become licensed and can handle the tasks required, men and women with a high school diploma as their highest level of educational advancement can still find job openings.

Increasingly, however, it is common for agents and brokers to hold college degrees. While some hold degrees in real estate, more common are degrees in business administration, marketing, finance, economics, or other fields. More details on the various educational options are provided in Chapter 14.

Of key importance is the need to be licensed. Because real estate transactions are complicated matters involving large amounts of money, it is important that those dealing with real estate professionals have some assurance they are receiving assistance from qualified individuals. As a result, it is standard practice that agents and brokers be licensed.

Licensing is controlled by the state in which one lives or practices business. Each state in the United States has its own licensing practices. Although they vary somewhat in their details, the overall approach tends to be similar from one state to the next. This includes several basic qualifications. Prospective real estate agents must be at least eighteen years old and have graduated from high school. To become licensed, they must pass a written examination. Such exams are less comprehensive for agents than for brokers, but in either case they include questions about state property laws, basic aspects of real estate transactions, and more. As a minimum educational requirement for a general sales license, prospective agents must have completed at least thirty hours of classroom instruction in most states; in some, the minimum requirement is ninety hours or more.

For licensing as a broker, most states require from sixty to ninety hours of classroom instruction, along with additional qualifications beyond those expected of agents. Usually these include previous experience in selling real estate (most typically one, two, or three years total) or in lieu of experience (in some states), a college degree with a major in real estate. Once licensed, real estate professionals must have their licenses renewed on a periodic basis.

While practices vary somewhat from state to state, it is illustrative to look at how one state, Colorado, determines qualifications of real estate brokers. The Colorado Real Estate Commission provides the following definition and explanation of licensing:

> Licensure is the process by which an agency of state government or other jurisdiction grants permission to individuals to engage in the practice of a particular profession, vocation, or occupation and prohibits all others from legally doing so. By ensuring a level of minimum competence, the licensure process protects the general public. It is the state regulatory agency's responsibility to establish the acceptable level of safe practice and to furnish the means for determining whether an individual meets that standard.

Like many other states, Colorado agencies use examinations as one of several methods to determine that individuals are qualified to practice as real estate brokers. That state's law recognizes three levels of responsibility and authority.

1. *Associate Broker.* This represents the entry-level license for real estate brokerage, with no previous active real estate licensure required. A person holding this designation may hold an inactive license, or may be employed and supervised by an employing broker.
2. *Independent Broker.* Two years of active licensure are required for this level of licensure. An independent broker may be inactive, or may be self-employed without employing other licensees.

Independent brokers may also practice under the supervision of employing brokers.

3. *Employing Broker.* An employing broker represents the highest level. A person with this designation may practice independently, or employ and supervise other licensees. An employing broker may also have an inactive licensure.

In addition to examination requirements, brokers must meet specific requirements for education and work experience. For instance, specified numbers of hours must be completed in areas such as real estate law and practice, trust accounts and record keeping, real estate closings, and practical applications.

Along with meeting training and licensing requirements, potential agents and brokers should also develop skills in communications and use of office technologies. Included within such skills should be the capability of using modern office and field technologies such as desktop computers, notebook computers, and personal digital assistants (PDAs), also known as handheld computers. Not long ago, such skills were not as frequently required of real estate professionals, especially those who might rely on secretaries or other office assistants for their own specialized skills, but they are becoming increasingly important today.

One Career Path

As an example of a career path in this area, consider the case of Christy, a North Carolina real estate agent. She started out in real estate as a secretary, and then worked her way up to agent's status.

Christy attended a community college and earned an associate degree in office systems technology, during which time she developed skills in word processing, business writing, office organization, and communication. While still in school she took a job as a part-time receptionist at a local real estate agency, and then made the transition to a full-time secretarial job at the same company two years later.

She enjoyed her role for a while, but as she gained experience she started feeling ambitions to do more. The work of the firm's agents appealed to her, and although they had training and experience that she lacked, Christy felt she could perform the same work if given the opportunity. She talked with her supervisor about that possibility, and he encouraged her to proceed. He made it clear that she could not expect an immediate job change, but if she obtained the proper credentials and passed the state licensing exam, he would have a place for her as an agent with his firm.

Christy began taking real estate classes, reading on her own, and doing everything she could to prepare for the state exam. Since she already worked in a real estate firm, she routinely encountered information and incidents that expanded her experience. When she met the minimum requirements for taking the real estate agent's exam, she took the test, and passed on her first attempt.

Once she started working as an agent, Christy found that what she suspected was true: she had a real flair for selling real estate. Her first sale was a small house in a neighborhood where property values were below average for her community, and the commission was not a large one, but she felt as though she had won the state lottery. She knew she was on her way.

During the first year, Christy did not sell as many houses as other agents in the company, but she was not discouraged. She realized that it can take time to build up contacts and develop a profile so that clients would be aware of her availability. In her second year her sales volume grew, and now, in her third year, she is confident about her future in real estate. Eventually, she hopes to become a broker. But even if she remains an agent for the foreseeable future, she enjoys her work and plans to remain in the field.

ADVANCEMENT POSSIBILITIES

A common way to advance in this field is simply to increase in the number of sales, the value of properties represented, or both. According to the U.S. Department of Labor, the median annual earnings of salaried real estate brokers, including commissions, top $45,000. It is not uncommon for this amount to exceed $80,000 yearly, and some brokers earn much more.

While agents and brokers may earn salaries, their primary source of income is commissions on sales. Thus incomes vary widely depending on the volume of properties sold and other factors. One of these is the rate of commission, which may vary according to agreements between agents and brokers, the sale price of property, and the type of property involved in a given transaction. For example, real estate professionals generally earn a higher percentage from the sale of commercial properties, unimproved land, or farms than they do in selling a private home.

Often, commissions are divided among several agents and brokers. In some cases those who list a property receive one portion, while another agent and broker who actually make the sale also receive their part of the commission. Generally the maximum amount is realized by those who list a property and then also close the sale.

Typically, experienced real estate agents earn higher incomes than those who are beginning their real estate careers. Experienced agents tend to have developed more contacts and have established a pattern of success that takes time to develop. Accordingly, beginning real estate professionals may need savings, a second income, or other resources to help while they become established in the field.

For those working as agents rather than brokers, median annual earnings are slightly more than $28,000, with earnings up to the mid-forties common, and some earning substantially more.

Since brokers earn higher incomes and may employ agents to expand their business, moving up to broker's status is a common method of advancement. As noted earlier, brokers must have sufficient training and experience to pass a special examination to achieve the designation of broker. This extra effort can be well worth making, however, from a career development standpoint.

Another approach is to progress from part-time to full-time real estate employment. Agents who follow this path use their experience to develop skills, build a base of potential future clients, and become better known in their communities. While real estate can provide a lucrative career, it can also challenge the resources and staying power of even the most dedicated person. Because of the many factors involved in buying and selling real estate, success is not always guaranteed even for hardworking, well-trained people. A downturn in the economy, excessive competition, or something as simple as buyers changing their minds can limit the number of successful sales transactions. As a result, some professionals find it impractical to pursue this type of work as their only source of income. Instead, they function as part-time agents, working during evenings or weekends or following some other type of less-than-full-time schedule. Then during other working hours, they work at another job on a part-time or full-time basis.

Other possibilities for advancement include moving into related areas such as investing, insurance, land development, property management, or a position as a corporate executive.

ADDITIONAL SOURCES OF INFORMATION

The National Association of Realtors has nearly eighty thousand members and, as such, is the field's largest trade association. Members include both residential and commercial realtors including brokers, salespeople, property managers, appraisers, counselors, and other real estate professionals. All members pledge to a strict code of ethics and standards of practice.

The association provides a wealth of information and services. A major goal is helping members become more profitable and successful. The organization fosters professional development, research, and exchange of information. Services include educational opportunities, publications, designations and certifications, and more.

For more details, contact:

National Association of Realtors
700 Eleventh Street NW
Washington, DC 20001
realtor.com

The following organizations offer further information on a career as a residential real estate agent or broker.

American Association of Small Property Owners
Georgetown Place
1101 Thirtieth Street NW, Suite 500
Washington, DC 20007
202-625-8330
smallpropertyowner.com

Council of Real Estate Brokerage Managers
430 North Michigan Avenue
Chicago, IL 60611
800-621-8738
crb.com

Women's Council of Realtors
430 North Michigan Avenue
Chicago, IL 60611
800-245-8512

3

COMMERCIAL, OFFICE, AND INDUSTRIAL REAL ESTATE

While the great majority of real estate brokers and agents focus on selling private homes, some specialize in commercial property. Generally speaking, commercial property consists of real estate that is used for producing income or related business purposes. Retail stores, parking lots, warehouses, office buildings, restaurants, shopping centers, malls, condominiums, apartment buildings, and other types of real estate fit into this category.

Some agents and brokers include commercial property as part of their business while specializing in the sale of residential property. A different approach is taken by those who focus primarily or exclusively on commercial property. They either sell such properties to those who desire ownership as a business investment, or use their skills in seeking clients to become tenants.

In many ways, working in commercial real estate is similar to the residential end of the field. It requires the expenditure of a great deal of time and energy in activities such as marketing properties and showing them to prospective buyers. At the same time, there are significant differences. Instead of dealing with families or individuals interested in buying a home, they cater to businesspeople who have an entirely different set of motivations. These clients are interested in property acquisitions for financial reasons, which can include not only the basic potential for making a profit, but also tax considerations and other factors involved in complex business transactions. Thus brokers and agents must be well informed.

A related area is that of industrial brokerage. Here, agents and brokers deal with a variety of properties used by industry such as production facilities, manufacturing plants, distribution sites, and warehouses. While such properties may not be as visible as office buildings or commercial property serving the general public, they represent an important part of the real estate industry. For discussion purposes, the areas of commercial, office, and industrial real estate are grouped together in this chapter since they share many common elements and are distinguished from residential brokerage in the business nature of the properties involved.

Here are some representative job descriptions for positions in the commercial real estate industry provided by the National Association of Industrial and Office Properties:

EXECUTIVE POSITIONS

Company's Chief Executive Officer (CEO). Has overall responsibility for guiding and directing all company operations and activities with the objective of achieving maximum profitability; establishes short- and long-term objectives, plans, policies, and standards. Reports to, and may be a member of, the board of directors.

Region/Division Head (multiple-office company). Has overall responsibility for guiding and directing all region/division operations and activities with the objective of achieving maximum profitability; establishes short- and long-term objectives. Reports to the chief operating officer.

Company's Chief Operating Officer (COO). Assists and supports the CEO in the overall direction of the company; establishes and implements operating procedures; plans and directs day-to-day operations and activities of the company; evaluates operating results for the CEO's review.

DEVELOPMENT POSITIONS

Company's Development Head. Has overall responsibility for the company's development activities. Establishes and implements development policies and strategies to support company objectives; identifies and evaluates development opportunities. Specific responsibilities may include market evaluation, identifying and acquiring sites, financial or cost analysis of proposed projects, participation in financing negotiations, coordinating activities with construction executive, and negotiating construction loans with prospective lenders. Generally reports to the chief operating officer.

Region/Division Development Head. Responsibilities are similar to those of the development head, but are limited to a specific region or division. Generally reports to the company's development head or the COO.

Business Development Head. Responsible for identifying commercial development opportunities; keeps current regarding area office markets and office development needs; follows up on development leads and contacts; participates in selection of financial sources, structuring deals, negotiation of legal documents, and architectural and construction planning. Resolves day-to-day problems and expedites and assures project completion according to specifications.

Senior Developer. Participates in commercial development activities. Has overall responsibility for assigned projects, which are often projects of an extremely complex nature.

Developer. Participates in commercial development activities. Responsibilities are generally limited to involvement in smaller or less complex projects than those of the senior developer.

FINANCIAL POSITIONS

Company's Chief Financial Officer. Responsible for the company's overall financial plans, policies, and practices; plans and directs treasury, budgeting and forecasting, audit, tax planning and reporting, and accounting activities. Develops and maintains relationships with banks and other sources of financing. Responsible for developing financing packages for development projects. Reports to the CEO.

Company's Controller. Responsible for the company's accounting practices, maintenance of fiscal records, and preparation of financial reports. Responsibilities include budgeting, forecasting, financial analysis, and financial control systems.

Region/Division Financial Head. Responsible for all aspects of the region's or division's financial plans and practices, including the business units within the division or region. Plans and directs budgeting and forecasting, audit, tax planning and reporting, and accounting activities. Typically reports to the chief financial officer or the company's controller.

Financial Manager. Responsible for a portion of the company's or region/division's accounting practices, records maintenance, and preparation of financial reports. Supervises financial analysts. May be involved in the negotiation of agreements involving land and buildings. Participates in the long-term planning process. Typically reports to the region/division financial head or to the company's CFO or controller.

Senior Project Controller. Responsible for financial and accounting matters relating to one or more specific projects; supervises other project controllers; monitors all accounting activities, audits, tax reporting and payments, and cash management; prepares or coordinates preparation of budgets and financial reports. May assist the CFO or region/division financial head in development project financing studies.

Project Controller. Responsible for financial and accounting matters relating to one or more specific projects; participates in assigned accounting activities, audits, tax reporting and payments, and cash management; may prepare or participate in preparation of budgets and financial reports. Assists in development of project financing studies as requested.

Financial Analyst. Responsible for providing financial analysis, development budgets, and accounting reports to management personnel. Evaluates present and proposed financial programs through statistical analysis and interpretation of short- and long-term trend data. Analyzes the financial feasibility of proposed development projects. Conducts market research to forecast and analyze trends of general business conditions. Analyzes the financial structure of proposed transactions. Participates in the review of new transactions and coordinates with others in the development of a financial plan.

Senior Financial Analyst. Works on the most complex projects.

Financial Analyst. Works on projects of moderate complexity.

Property Accountant. Responsible for cash management, general ledger accounting, and financial reporting for one or more properties.

ASSET MANAGEMENT AND ACQUISITIONS POSITIONS

Asset Management Head. Responsible for maximizing the performance and value of the company's portfolio of real estate assets that are owned and/or managed through acquisitions, dispositions, operations, and so on. Has responsibility for formulating and implementing a long-range real estate asset management strategy.

Region/Division Asset Management Head. Responsible for maximizing the performance and value of a region's or division's portfolio of real estate assets that are owned and/or managed through acquisitions, dispositions, operations, and so on.

Acquisitions and Dispositions Head. Responsible for the activities of both of the following positions.

Acquisitions Head. Responsible for identifying and analyzing acquisitions opportunities and negotiating transactions for clients, the company, or the business unit.

Dispositions Head. Responsible for identifying and analyzing disposition opportunities and negotiating transactions for clients, the company, or the business unit.

MARKETING POSITIONS

Marketing Head. Responsible for generating and maintaining prospective tenants' interest; negotiating or participating in the negotiation of legal documents; coordinating the planning and construction or renovation of space with the tenant construction coordinator; conducting advertising and promotional campaigns to ensure project exposure.

MANAGEMENT INFORMATION SYSTEMS/ INFORMATION TECHNOLOGY POSITIONS

MIS/IT Head. Responsible for the company's computer information technology including strategic planning, application and systems development, and computer operations. Develops the company's technologic architecture and standards. Develops and manages the company's MIS budget. Establishes and maintains strategic vendor relationships.

LEGAL POSITIONS

Legal Head. Primarily responsible for reviewing the legal aspects of all financial documents and contracts; maintains familiarity with legal requirements in locations where the company is operating; serves as liaison with outside counsel.

CONSTRUCTION POSITIONS

Construction Head. Responsible for establishing the company's engineering and construction standards for all construction and/or development projects; ensures that construction work meets or exceeds standards within cost estimates; provides technical advice and expertise regarding feasibility of proposed projects; monitors quality and quantity of work performed on projects in progress. Reports to the chief executive officer or chief operating officer.

Region/Division Construction Head. Responsible for ensuring that the region's or division's construction work meets or exceeds engineering and construction standards within cost estimates; provides technical advice and expertise regarding feasibility of proposed projects; monitors quality and quantity of work performed on projects in progress. Typically reports to the company's construction head or to development head.

Business Unit Construction Head. Responsible for ensuring that the business unit's construction work meets or exceeds standards within cost estimates; provides technical advice and expertise regarding feasibility of proposed projects; monitors quality and quantity of work performed on projects in progress. Typically reports to the region/division construction head or the business unit's head. (Note: a business unit's management reports to a region/division head or to the top real estate management. A business unit has no subordinate business units reporting to it.)

Construction Project Manager. Responsible for the overall direction of assigned construction projects, including review of and recommendations on planning and design, contract negotiations, day-to-day on-site progress and activities; may participate in obtaining relevant permits from local, state, and government agencies. Has the highest level of responsibility for individual projects.

Tenant Construction Coordinator. Responsible for coordinating construction of tenant space within one or more facilities; provides periodic on-site supervision of tenant construction to ensure consistency with desires of owner; sets goals, reviews plans, obtains bids, estimates costs, inspects and approves completed project.

PROPERTY MANAGEMENT POSITIONS

Property Management Head. Responsible for the operation and maintenance of all physical facilities owned or managed by the company, including establishing and monitoring budget, ensuring efficiency of physical plant, sustaining mechanical and cosmetic maintenance and preservation or renovation of facility, supervising contract services, and maintaining good working relationships with tenants. Typically reports to the chief executive officer or chief operating officer.

Region/Division Property Management Head. Responsible for the operation and maintenance of the region's or division's physical facilities owned or managed; may include establishing and monitoring budget, ensuring efficiency of physical plant, sustaining mechanical and cosmetic maintenance and preservation or renovation of facility, managing contract services, and maintaining good working relationships with tenants. Typically reports to the company's property management head or to the company's development head.

Property Manager. Has operational responsibility of one or more properties. Responsibilities include collecting rents, maintaining grounds, interfacing with tenants, and preparing annual budgets. May have P&L (profit and loss) responsibility. Property managers are typically on-site and may or may not have leasing responsibilities. Typically reports to the region/division property management head or to the company's property management head.

Assistant Property Manager. Assists the property manager with the day-to-day operations of the properties. Performs rent-collecting duties when necessary; may show apartments to prospective tenants.

Tenant Relations Manager. Establishes and maintains positive relations with tenants; listens and responds to their comments. Helps resolve tenant/management conflicts. Promotes general goodwill between tenants and property managers.

Facility Manager. Operates specific properties on a day-to-day basis. Directs contract workforce for maintenance and operation of physical plant in such areas as janitorial work and electrical and mechanical systems. Maintains working relationship with tenants. Maintains emergency preparedness procedures.

BROKERAGE AND LEASING POSITIONS

Brokerage Head. Responsible for all commercial, industrial, and land sales and commercial leasing activities of the company.

Region/Division Brokerage Head. Responsible for all commercial, industrial, and land sales and leasing activities of the region or division.

Broker. Responsible for negotiating and closing commercial, industrial, and/or land sales and leasing deals.

Lease Administrator. Responsible for providing analysis and support for property management, facility planning, lease administration, and financial reporting. Participates in real estate transactions including lease negotiation and administration. Conducts analyses of leased and owned properties. Provides budget, financial, and status reports to management. Tracks lease information, property values, capital expenditures, rental rates, and real estate assignments.

Leasing Representative. Responsible for identifying and contacting prospective tenants; participates in or conducts lease negotiations for one or more new projects or for available space in existing projects.

THE PEOPLE WITH WHOM COMMERCIAL, OFFICE, AND INDUSTRIAL BROKERS WORK

Real estate agents, brokers, and others who specialize in commercial properties interact with people from a wide range of backgrounds. Unlike those working in residential real estate, their primary contacts fall within the business world. Their clients may include corporate executives, small business owners, investment specialists, and other businesspeople. They may also deal with other brokers, mortgage officers, insurance representatives, government officials, attorneys, property managers, land developers, and other professionals in areas related to real estate.

In addition to clients and potential clients, agents and brokers work with various support personnel such as office assistants, secretaries, accounting specialists, and other staff. They may also maintain contacts with other businesspeople such as peer members of professional associations and local business leaders.

THE SETTINGS IN WHICH COMMERCIAL, OFFICE, AND INDUSTRIAL BROKERS WORK

Like those who specialize in residential real estate, commercial brokers spend much of their time working in offices. Such environments are generally quite comfortable, offering pleasant surroundings conducive to reading, writing reports or correspondence, talking on the phone, working with computers, or meeting with clients or colleagues.

Within these settings, they may operate a variety of equipment including desktop or notebook computers, printers, fax machines, and sophisticated telephone systems. Some may also utilize advanced technologies for videoconferencing or other communications.

Frequently, brokers and others who work in this area perform work outside of the office setting. They visit properties that may be handled by their firms, travel to meet with clients or conduct background work, show properties to prospective buyers, and travel for other reasons. While on-site, they may walk or ride around outdoors, walk through buildings, and spend time looking about properties or showing them to clients. In the process, they may put in a great deal of time in automobiles, airplanes, or other modes of transportation, as well as in hotel rooms while on the road.

Some brokers and other professionals in this field work more than the standard forty-hour week, especially during peak periods when major deals are in the works. At other times, they may enjoy flexibility in setting work schedules or taking time off.

TRAINING AND OTHER QUALIFICATIONS

Like residential brokerage, work as a commercial agent or broker requires good communication skills and an ability to get along well with people. But it also necessitates a higher level of technical business knowledge, according to the National Association of Industrial and Office Properties (NAIOP), with successful commercial agents often holding a bachelor's degree or a graduate degree in business. A strong educational background is needed to support work with corporations, tenants, institutional buyers and sellers, and a wide variety of businesses and other organizations. As pointed out by NAIOP, the majority of commercial agents specialize in a specific type of property. For example, an agent might focus on industrial, office, or retail property, or on hotels, apartments, or recreational property.

To qualify as an agent or broker, the same basic factors apply as with residential brokerage. Most importantly, they must be licensed by the state in which they work. This requires passing a written test, which is more comprehensive for brokers than for agents, as well as completing instruction in basic real estate areas.

In commercial real estate, a college degree is more frequently required than in the residential area. Many professionals hold master's degrees or other advanced educational credentials. Due to the complex nature of many business transactions, a background in accounting, finance, law, or other technical area can be particularly helpful.

Once employed in the field, some brokers and other real estate personnel earn special certifications from professional associations. These certifications help demonstrate competency to clients and peers.

Desirable personal traits include solid analytical skills, strong abilities in oral and written communication, and an aggressive approach to completing work tasks. Good "people skills" are essential.

ADDITIONAL SOURCES OF INFORMATION

The following organizations offer further information on careers in commercial, office, and industrial real estate.

National Association of Industrial and Office Properties
An excellent source of information is the National Association of Industrial and Office Properties (NAIOP). The association, which boasts some ten thousand members, offers a variety of services including forums on

topics such as build-to-suit development, business park development, capital markets, industrial development, investment management, mixed-use development, and office development.

The association also provides information on industry trends, research studies, legislative issues, and association news. Its publications include *DEVELOPMENT* magazine, two online newsletters, compensation reports, and educational audiotapes.

In addition to its services to professional members, this organization has a membership category for students and maintains a career center offering the following resources:

- A web "jobsite" where those seeking jobs may post résumés and search job openings for free
- Links to U.S. and Canadian universities offering real estate programs
- Real estate career information including detailed descriptions of careers in real estate, information on real estate skills and career paths, career information from the *Wall Street Journal,* compensation information, and employee selection advice

For more information, contact:

National Association of Industrial and Office Properties
2201 Cooperative Way, Suite 300
Herndon, VA 20171
703-904-7100
naiop.org

Society of Industrial and Office Realtors

A great resource for those interested in this area is the Society of Industrial and Office Realtors, a major professional commercial and industrial real estate association. It has over 2,200 members in twenty countries and focuses on serving commercial real estate brokerage specialists. The society is a professional affiliate of the National Association of Realtors.

Members of this organization may qualify for the SIOR (Specialist, Industrial and Office Real Estate) designation, which is a professional symbol indicating a high level of knowledge, production, and ethics.

In addition to certification, the society provides a variety of professional services. It fosters personal networking among commercial real estate brokers, independent industrial/office property brokers, corporate real estate executives, and others with an interest in this area. The society also publishes a quarterly magazine and other helpful publications. Of special note is its *Executive Guide to Specialists in Industrial and Office Real Estate,* which is widely considered to be the "blue book" among commercial real estate professionals.

The organization also offers educational courses and seminars, public relations services, mediation and arbitration services for resolving business disputes, and other helpful programs and services.

For more information, contact:

Society of Industrial and Office Realtors
National Association of Realtors
700 Eleventh Street NW
Washington, DC 20001
202-737-1150
realtor.com

CREW Network

An organization of special interest to women is the CREW Network, an association serving women in the commercial real estate industry. With a membership of five thousand professionals, the group represents all aspects of the commercial real estate industry including brokerage, law, leasing, financing, property management, and acquisitions.

Many members of this organization are presidents, CEOs, owners, partners, or senior managers in their companies. About 3 percent of the organization's members are men.

Services provided by the CREW Network include business development resources; leadership training; educational opportunities; and a job bank, known as Career Connections, where commercial real estate–related jobs are listed.

In addition, the association sponsors the CREW Foundation, a nonprofit charitable arm of the CREW Network that provides grants to benefit women's and girls' programs that promote economic self-sufficiency and self-determination.

For more information, contact:

CREW Network
1201 Wakarusa Drive
Lawrence, KS 66049-3803
785-832-1808

C H A P T E R 4

FARM AND LAND BROKERAGE

The history of civilization is tightly linked with the development of farming. It was not until human beings began to master agriculture that civilized societies as we know them began to emerge. For many centuries, the great majority of rural residents lived on farms. In the last century, however, advancing industrialization and the growth not only of cities but also suburban areas made places other than farms the more common dwelling places. At the same time, the number of people working on farms has also dropped.

According to the U.S. Department of Agriculture, in the last forty years the number of farms has dropped from 5.8 million to 2.1 million. About five million people, less than 10 percent of the rural population, now live on farms.

At the same time, farms are as important as ever in providing the food that everyone in our society needs. Former farmland may have value for other purposes. And the value of the property in many rural areas has increased markedly, making this an area within the real estate industry that can be very attractive for those with the right training and experience.

THE NATURE OF THE WORK

Agents and brokers who work with farms, ranches, and other large properties perform many of the same functions as those who deal with other types of real estate. They seek out agreements to place properties for sale (or listings), and then follow up with details such as determining competitive market prices, arranging for title searches, and showing properties to potential buyers. A major responsibility is familiarizing themselves with the advantages of any property so they can make it sound attractive to potential buyers. For example, they might memorize details such as what crops have been grown on the land in the last ten years, and master figures on crop production.

Agents and brokers also spend time setting up meetings between buyers and sellers, and helping work out details of transactions in which farms or other properties are sold. In some cases, they may help to arrange financing for a prospective buyer. They may also take major responsibility for closing sales, or may work with lenders or attorneys in completing this process.

Brokers may supervise agents and clerical staff. They also manage their own offices, market their business, and take care of other matters necessary in running a business. Some agents and brokers focus all or most of their energies on farms and rural properties. Others handle a more diverse array of properties. Some also perform other types of work along with their real estate business. For example, they may practice law or sell insurance.

After an agreement has been reached, agents and brokers see that any special terms of the contract are met. This may include inspecting houses or other buildings for pest infestations, identifying needed repairs, and seeing that repairs are carried out before the closing date.

To some extent, the nature of the work depends on the size and type of properties being represented. Some agents specialize in very large farms, ranches, or other properties. Others focus on smaller farms.

According to the U.S. Department of Agriculture, nine out of ten farms in this country qualify as small farms, meaning they generate $250,000 or less in gross sales. Many smaller farms are proprietorships, partnerships, or family corporations. Many larger farms are organized as non-family corporations or cooperatives. Such distinctions are important to real estate professionals as they affect not just the potential of farms for sale to others, but also the business agreements involved.

Obviously, a primary purpose of farms is raising crops, livestock, or both. But they also meet other purposes. For example, some farms serve as retirement farms, where people live after retiring from either farming or other careers, including those totally unrelated to agriculture. These farms may have profit-making as an incentive, but if so it tends to be only a part of the reason residents have chosen to live there. At least as important is the quality of life involved. Factors such as the condition of a house located on the property may be of more importance to potential buyers for this type of farm than for those with a purely commercial interest.

Other farms consist of what the USDA refers to as residential/lifestyle farms. For these farms, the operators have a major occupation other than farming. They may view farming as a hobby. Or the farm may serve as a place of residence while supplementing their primary income. In some cases, it is a start toward the future, involving plans for eventual full-time farming.

Another category recognized by the Department of Agriculture is that of "farming occupation" farms. Here, operators pursue farming as their major occupation. While the household may receive additional income from nonfarm work (such as a job held by a spouse), the major source of income is the operation of the farm itself.

Regardless of the type of farm, one factor setting it off from some other types of real estate is the potential to generate sales. The government groups farms into several categories based on this factor. Low-sales farms are those "farming occupation" farms with sales less than $100,000, while high-sales farms are those "farming occupation" farms with sales between $100,000 and $249,999. In addition, large family farms have sales between $250,000 and $499,999, and very large family farms have sales of $500,000 or more.

Even though most American farms are classified as small family farms, agricultural production is heavily concentrated among large family farms, very large family farms, and non-family farms, according to the USDA. Together they constitute less than 10 percent of all farms, but account for more than two-thirds of agricultural production in the United States.

From a real estate angle, larger farms offer tremendous earnings potential. With sale prices often in the multimillion-dollar range, they provide possibilities for hefty commissions. The same is true to a lesser degree for smaller farms as well. Of course the number of farms sold each year is much smaller than that of private residences, and competition within this market can be steep.

THE PEOPLE WITH WHOM FARM AND LAND BROKERS WORK

Real estate agents and brokers who specialize in rural and agricultural property interact with a wide variety of people. Their clients may include farmers, ranchers, agricultural firms, investors, small companies, or large corporations. On a peer basis, they may deal with mortgage officers or other bank officials, attorneys, other real estate professionals, or local government officials.

Clients come from all kinds of backgrounds. They may represent traditional farming families or be newcomers to the agricultural community. Some are primarily interested in business investments, while others may be interested in farms or other properties for recreational or retirement purposes.

Within the office setting, agents and brokers may work with receptionists, secretaries, other agents, or other personnel. They also may maintain contacts throughout the business community, participating in civic clubs or other organizations where they mingle with people from a wide range of business and professional backgrounds.

THE SETTINGS IN WHICH FARM AND LAND BROKERS WORK

Like other real estate agents and brokers, those who specialize in this field tend to spend a good deal of time in their offices, which normally provide a comfortable working environment. While the size and type of office setting varies, the norm is a comfortable setting with attractive furniture; adequate lighting, ventilation, and temperature controls; and a generally pleasant environment. In addition, office environments generally include modern equipment such as computers, printers, and fax machines.

In some cases, home offices are used instead of traditional offices. Here, agents and brokers take advantage of E-mail, the Internet, and other advances in electronic communications to make home-based offices highly practical and efficient.

Of course all work in this field does not take place in offices. Agents and brokers spend significant time visiting farms or other properties, whether this means familiarizing themselves with new listings, meeting new clients, or showing properties to prospective buyers. While on-site, they may walk around properties, look through buildings, and generally move about. In addition, they also put in many hours in automobiles as they travel to and from sites they are endeavoring to sell.

As with other agents and brokers, some professionals in this field work more than the standard forty-hour week. They may frequently work during evenings and weekends to make themselves available to clients. At the same time, they often enjoy flexibility in taking time off and setting daily work schedules.

TRAINING AND OTHER QUALIFICATIONS

Agents and brokers must have the same types of qualifications in the farm and rural property area as are required in more general real estate sales. This includes being licensed by the state in which they work, which requires passing a written test. Separate tests are involved for agents and brokers, with the latter being more comprehensive. Before taking such tests, prospective agents and brokers must take classes about the laws covering real estate transactions and related facets of the real estate profession. In some cases, this involves taking a series of classes or seminars focusing only on preparation for the appropriate exam. An alternative approach is to complete college courses as part of a real estate degree program or a component within a business or finance program (see Chapter 14 for more details on educational preparation). Certain experience requirements also apply for those who want to become brokers, although in some states they may be waived for those who have earned a bachelor's degree in real estate.

While a college degree is not necessarily required, many firms prefer to hire college graduates, and more and more agents and brokers have some college training if not a degree. Most professionals in this field find value in having completed courses in business, English, computing, and other areas as well as in real estate. Courses in agriculture or farm management can be particularly useful for those working in farm and land brokerage.

Educational preparation aside, a familiarity with farms and rural communities is necessary for success in this field. Those who have grown up in such surroundings may have an inherent advantage, but others may gain familiarity by studying diligently, interacting with farmers and farm families, and traveling or living in communities where agriculture is dominant.

Personal qualifications include good skills in oral communication, the ability to get along well with others, and an outgoing personality. Honesty, maturity, and a trustworthy nature are also important.

To help you envision how a real estate agent or broker might get started in this area, consider the early career of Bruce, a broker based in Des Moines, Iowa.

Bruce is a college graduate with a degree in business administration. His grandfather and several other relatives had been full-time farmers, so he always felt he had a connection to the farming community even though Bruce himself had never worked as a farmer. He grew up in farm country and felt generally knowledgeable about the agriculture business. So after graduating from college, his job search included looking at jobs that had some connection to farming.

Bruce had never thought much about working in real estate, though, until a family friend asked if he wanted to work with his real estate firm the summer after his junior year at Iowa State University. Bruce took the job, and at first most of his duties were mundane ones. He performed general help around the office, filled in for the receptionist while she was on vacation, put up "for sale" signs for properties represented by the firm, and took care of other responsibilities. Although this company did not specialize in farms or other large properties, it did conduct some business in this area. As he encountered clients and heard discussions related to transactions involving farms, it occurred to Bruce that his long-standing familiarity with agriculture and his budding interest in the real estate business might be combined as he pursued career plans.

This thinking prompted him to enroll in two real estate courses during his senior year. He had not yet decided that this would be a definite career path, but held it out as one possibility among others. One consideration was that he found the content of the real estate courses to be interesting and felt that additional course work or training might be something to pursue in the future.

Shortly before graduation, Bruce landed several job interviews, and ended up taking a position with an insurance company. But after graduation and within a few weeks of starting that job, Bruce realized it wasn't for him.

The idea of working in real estate came back to him, and he decided to follow up on it. So he did some groundwork and identified several companies that dealt with real estate. He contacted each of them, and one broker seemed particularly interested in giving him an opportunity. So he hired Bruce on a provisional basis. Bruce worked as a nonlicensed agent, performing basic duties while learning on the job and completing short-term classes offered specifically for preparation for the required state exam.

Bruce passed his exam on the first attempt and the rest, as they say, is history. He is now a successful agent specializing in the farm market, and is considering moving up to broker status. He enjoys his job, and his future looks bright.

ADVANCEMENT POSSIBILITIES

There are a number of ways in which agents and brokers in this area may advance. Many of them are similar to the career paths of other real estate professionals.

For agents, a common path is to progress to the status of broker. A broker may own his or her own firm and may become progressively more successful by expanding the size of the business as gauged by number of listings or annual sales.

For both agents and brokers, advancement may consist of continued success in terms of the volume of sales or the types of deals closed. Or it might mean expanding into other areas such as insurance, investments, property management, real estate counseling, or other areas.

In another direction, advancement for some agents or brokers might entail taking the corporate path. For example, an agent's contacts might lead to employment with a large land-acquisition firm or agricultural company.

ADDITIONAL SOURCE OF INFORMATION

National Association of Realtors
700 Eleventh Street NW
Washington, DC 20001

CHAPTER

5

REAL ESTATE APPRAISING

An important function within the real estate field is that of appraising. This is the process of determining the condition and value of houses, business structures, farms, or other types of real estate.

THE NATURE OF THE WORK

Appraisers make careful examinations of property and then document their findings, which are then used for a variety of purposes. In a typical example, the value of a house that is being sold must be determined not only so the buyer will be assured the price is fair, but also so that a mortgage lender has sufficient information on which to loan the necessary funds. If a bank made a loan for $100,000 but the property was worth only $85,000, then the bank would risk substantial losses if the borrower failed to meet repayment obligations and the bank was forced to reclaim the property.

Similarly, insurance companies rely on appraisals in establishing the value of property they insure, and local governments may use such information in determining the amount of taxes to assess on privately owned property. Such values may also be useful in everything from bankruptcy or divorce proceedings to establishing the value of inheritances.

Appraisers thus play an important role. They make site visits to the property in question, closely examine its condition, and complete reports documenting their findings.

According to the American Society of Appraisers, some examples of the impact appraisers have on citizens include the following:

- Playing a role in determining the amount of taxes paid on homes
- Helping determine whether mortgages or other loans should be granted
- Helping set prices for personal residences, businesses, farms, and other property
- Determining the value of property donated to charities or tax-exempt organizations

While many appraisers specialize in real estate, others work in other areas. They appraise gems and jewelry, machinery and equipment, aircraft, antiques, works of art, and other types of property. Most men and women who work in real estate appraising, however, do not address these areas. Instead, they focus on real estate, often specializing in a specific type of real estate.

Within the real estate area, property falls into several categories. Some appraisers focus on just one area, while others may cover several.

Those dealing with urban properties, for example, may deal with residential property, commercial property, or both. Residential property may include single-family homes, townhouses, or condominiums, while commercial properties may include shopping centers, office buildings, warehouses, manufacturing facilities, hospitals, schools, or a variety of other properties.

Appraisers dealing with rural properties may appraise farms, ranches, orchards, vineyards, rural business properties, or other properties outside urban settings.

Some appraisers are involved with other specific areas such as evaluating timber and timberland or assessing all taxable property within a given government jurisdiction.

Because land values are subject to frequent change, the work of appraisers is highly important. By providing expert estimates and analyses of property's market value, they support various real estate–related processes including the purchase or sale of property, estate planning, financial planning, leasing or renting, and tax planning.

Typical tasks performed by appraisers include describing land, noting and evaluating property improvements, discussing future use of property, and estimating its value. The latter may include making comparisons with similar properties, estimating the costs needed to duplicate a property, and considering probable income generated by the property.

Appraisers spend a significant portion of their time preparing written appraisal reports. Such reports must conform to certain expectations regarding both content and style, and their development requires a diligent and professional approach. Experienced professionals realize that this is one of the most important functions performed by those undertaking the appraisal process.

Once appraisers obtain all the necessary information, the written report becomes the "product" they deliver to clients. These reports are then used by others in making decisions about property transactions. Home owners or real estate professionals representing them, for instance, use such information in deciding the asking price in selling a house. Prospective buyers, at the same time, rely on appraisal reports for assurance that they are not being overcharged in property acquisitions. Such information is also used by lenders, insurance companies, and others.

Appraisal reports contain several types of information. This typically includes a description of the property in question, a statement of the kind of value being assessed (such as fair market value or the cost needed to replace it), and the procedures employed to arrive at estimated property value. Such reports also include information about the appraiser and a signature attesting to the validity of the information presented.

According to the American Society of Farm Managers and Rural Appraisers, some elements of a narrative report include:

- Identification of the property being appraised
- Purpose of the appraisal
- Effective date of appraisal
- Definition of estate under appraisal
- County, regional, and neighborhood data
- Description of subject property
- Correlation and conclusions

- Highest and best use, market approach, income approach, cost approach
- Certificate of appraiser
- Maps, charts, photos
- General information such as the report format, explanations, and data presentation

For appraisers, the challenges of the job vary with the type of property being evaluated. For example, consider a piece of property that is made up of wetlands. These areas not only involve difficulties in preparation for practical use, but also require special consideration from an environmental viewpoint. Typically, any plans for using such property must include a complex process involving obtaining appropriate permits and demonstrating the degree of any environmental impact. Thus for appraisers, arriving at land values includes weighing factors not normally considered with more ordinary properties.

Similarly, appraising historic properties offers a different set of challenges. Here, more emphasis may be placed on exterior appearance and the need to maintain consistency within a neighborhood than with other types of property.

Whatever the specialty area involved, a major consideration in the work of appraisers is the matter of ethics. Appraisers must take great care to be objective in their efforts. When assessing the value of any property, they must not be influenced by the needs or desires of their clients. At the same time, it is considered unethical to accept fees based on a percentage of the appraised value of property, for this might encourage appraisers to inflate the value of property so their fees would be higher. Still another standard is that appraisers should not have a personal financial interest in property they work with, except in cases where they have fully disclosed such interests to their clients.

THE PEOPLE WITH WHOM APPRAISERS WORK

Appraisers serve a variety of clients, according to the American Society of Farm Managers and Rural Appraisers (ASFMRA), including property owners, operators, attorneys, bankers, insurance and mortgage companies, and government agencies.

Generally, variety in terms of contact with people is the norm. Appraisers may deal with home owners from a wide range of backgrounds, including those for whom the appraisal process is a new experience as well as those more experienced with real estate–related transactions. They may also work with business owners and managers, real estate agents, insurance agents, and others.

At the same time, it is important to realize that appraisers may spend a significant portion of their time working alone, whether in the field or in their offices. With the latter, they may also share work space with other appraisers, and may interact with secretaries or other staff.

THE SETTINGS IN WHICH APPRAISERS WORK

One advantage many appraisers see with their field is the variety they experience in daily work environments. Their work combines both visiting the properties they appraise and putting in time in their offices. While working in the field, appraisers enjoy a tremendous amount of variety. An appraiser specializing in residential work, for example, may move from a cottage to a mansion, encountering different people and varying environmental conditions.

Appraisers also work in offices where they schedule appraisal visits; write reports; and answer letters, telephone calls, or E-mail messages. To complete such work, they may employ computers, fax machines, computer printers, and other types of office equipment.

Appraisers also spend a good deal of time traveling to and from the sites where they complete the appraisal process.

For rural appraisers, the daily routine often includes a significant amount of time walking and standing, and putting in time both indoors and outdoors. Sometimes harsh weather is a factor. According to the ASFMRA, typical attire during this process is less likely to be a business suit than jeans, sport clothes, and boots.

One determining factor in the work environment is the type of employer. Some appraisers operate their own small businesses or work as part of a small firm specializing in appraising services. Often called fee appraisers, they work directly for clients on a contract basis.

Others are employed by organizations such as insurance companies, banks, or other companies involved in buying or selling property. They are generally known as staff appraisers.

While many appraisers are employed in the private sector, public sector positions are also available. For example, the city of Red Deer, Alberta, recently advertised a position opening as a Senior Property Assessor/ Appraiser. Responsibilities for this position focus on assessing and appraising high-value and complex properties. Applicants were expected to have at least six years of experience, with certifications in real property assessment and an interest in working with commercial and industrial properties.

TRAINING AND OTHER QUALIFICATIONS

In an informal sense, virtually all real estate agents and brokers appraise property. As they look at properties and represent them for others, they gain the ability to make rough estimates of value. Thus moving into a formal role as an appraiser may be a natural role for some people who start out as real estate agents.

Working as an agent or broker is not a requirement for becoming an appraiser, however. In most states appraisers must hold a real estate license, and to gain such a license, they must have completed basic real estate instruction and have passed a written examination.

Completing real estate appraising courses with a college degree program or a privately offered real estate program is a good way to gain initial preparation in this field. A bachelor's degree in business or a related field can be helpful, especially if it provides background in areas such as taxation, finance, management, and use of computers.

Once they gain work experience in the field, appraisers may seek professional accreditation. Here, an organization such as the American Society of Appraisers (ASA) certifies a specific status indicating a certain level of professional preparation and competence. For example, the ASA designates professionals in two categories: Accredited Member or Accredited Senior Appraiser. For the former designation, requirements include at least two years of full-time appraisal experience, or the equivalent, in addition to successful completion of written and oral examinations covering topics such as principles and ethics of appraising, general valuation theory, and technical expertise. To obtain the Accredited Senior Appraiser designation, at least five years of full-time work experience is required, along with the other criteria.

The ASA offers a number of courses, seminars, and other educational opportunities related to appraising. Perhaps most helpful are the ASA's principles of valuation courses related to real property.

The most basic course is Real Property Appraisal Theory, Principles and Concepts. It covers topics such as general valuation theory and principles; the three approaches to estimating value; steps of the appraisal process; factors affecting value; land valuation: highest and best use; adjustments and extractions; and property inspection techniques. Completion of the course requires twenty-seven contact hours and a three-hour exam.

Other helpful courses include the following:

- *Introduction to Income Capitalization* covers topics such as residual analysis techniques, compound interest functions, discounting and annuities, financial statements and ratio analysis, reconstruction of income streams, and income property classification.
- *Advanced Income Capitalization* deals with advanced topics including investment analysis, valuation of mortgage and equity, and cash equivalency and adjustments.
- *Urban Case Studies I* addresses case studies and the market appraisal report, emphasizing components, organization, composition, and supplemental exhibits.
- *Urban Case Studies II* covers the written appraisal report, analyzing data, adjustment techniques, narrated reports, and form reports.

The association also sponsors advanced courses in the real property area including the following:

- Applied Residential Property Valuation focuses on a number of topics including current theories and contemporary interpretations; techniques in collecting, analyzing, and interpreting data; the various factors involved in typical single-family residences, condominiums, and luxury homes; and problems in appraisals related to employee relocation.

- Applied Small Residential Income Property Valuation deals with topics such as inspection techniques, lender requirements, correct adjustment techniques, and the three traditional approaches to estimating value.
- Principles of Rural Appraisal covers annuity capitalization, direct and straight-line capitalization, and more.
- Advanced Rural Appraisal deals with the cost approach (breakdown of depreciation into physical, functional, and external components), income approach (band of investments, gross rent multipliers, and other factors), and sales comparison approach, and case studies using the different approaches.
- Appraisal Report Writing provides a look at various aspects of the process of writing appraisal reports including student writing exercises.

Many colleges and universities offer one or two courses in appraising as part of a real estate program or track. In addition, some institutions offer comprehensive programs related to appraising. For example, Lindenwood University in St. Charles, Missouri, offers a bachelor's degree program in valuation sciences, as well as a master's degree in the same field. In addition to its own courses, Lindenwood has an arrangement in place through which college credits will be awarded to those who successfully complete principles of valuation courses offered by the ASA.

For more information, contact:

Valuation Sciences Program
Lindenwood University
400 North Kingshighway
St. Charles, MO 63301

ADVANCEMENT POSSIBILITIES

Possibilities for advancement in the area of appraising vary. For staff appraisers, a workable approach is to remain with one employer and move up within the same organization to senior status. Not only can this lead to progressively higher salaries as time passes, but in some organizations it may be possible to advance to a supervisory role. Such a position might entail supervising other inspectors, or it might eventually involve moving into other types of management positions. Additional education or training in management techniques may be necessary for such a move.

Appraisers can also move from one employer to another, using their background and experience to gain a higher-paying job or an otherwise more desirable position. For instance, an appraiser employed by a small firm might take a position with a larger company.

Another possibility would be for a staff appraiser to start his or her own appraising business. In this instance, the challenges of running a small business could provide a stimulating career change.

ADDITIONAL SOURCES OF INFORMATION

The ASA offers a helpful brochure, *Questions and Answers About the Appraisal Profession*, which provides information about the profession. It includes details on the nature of appraising, specialized fields of appraising, where to find an appraiser, judging an appraiser's qualifications, ethical considerations, key points of appraisal reports, length of time appraisals may be considered up-to-date, types of expert advice available on appraising, and questions to ask when interviewing an appraiser.

For a free copy of this publication, contact:

American Society of Appraisers
P.O. Box 17265
Washington, DC 20041
800-ASU-VALU
appraisers.org

Another excellent source of information about this field is the ASFMRA, which serves not only rural appraisers but also farm managers, review appraisers, and agricultural consultants. The association's many educational opportunities include the chance to earn special designations such as Accredited Rural Appraiser and Real Property Review Appraiser.

For more information, contact:

American Society of Farm Managers and Rural Appraisers
950 South Cherry Street, Suite 508
Denver, CO 80246-2664
303-758-3513
asfmra.org

CHAPTER 6

PROPERTY MANAGEMENT

While most home owners take care of their own property, this is not typically the case in the business world. Instead, individuals or companies who own rental property and many other types of real estate rely on paid staff to provide day-to-day management of their property. The owners use such property as an investment or a source of income, and it is in their best interests to see that the property is properly maintained. Thus a continuing need exists for managers who take care of such matters. Some, typically called property managers or real estate managers, provide oversight for commercial real estate or for residential properties designed to produce income. Others, known as community association managers, oversee the management of community associations, condominiums, or similar properties.

In some cases, property or real estate managers are employed directly by the property owners. In others, they are employed by a property management firm and placed with clients through a contractual arrangement.

THE NATURE OF THE WORK

Property management may involve any of a number of different functions. For example, one Michigan firm specializes in assisting commercial property owners whose holdings consist of apartment buildings or complexes, office buildings, and strip centers. Its services include leasing services; bill payment; coordination of records related to insurance, utilities, property taxes, insurance, and other expenses; maintenance, cleaning, and repair services; and preparation of computer-generated status reports.

One of the most common jobs in this field is that of residential on-site manager. Managers of this type work at privately owned apartment complexes, government-assisted housing complexes, retirement facilities, condominiums, or other residential properties. In many cases, managers or assistant managers in this category actually live on-site, although this practice varies widely.

Other on-site managers work at nonresidential properties such as shopping centers or office buildings.

Some typical position titles in this field are as follows:

- Assistant property manager
- Building coordinator
- Building manager
- Lease administrator
- Property manager
- Senior property manager
- Vice president of property management
- Government property manager

Typical duties of property managers include handling financial matters such as paying mortgages, filing tax forms, arranging for insurance and paying insurance premiums, processing payroll information for custodians and other personnel, and processing maintenance bills. Some property managers also prepare financial reports and keep owners updated regarding matters such as lease renewals and occupancy rates.

Managers also arrange for services such as trash removal, snow removal, mowing and other grounds keeping, security, and custodial services. In some cases this involves hiring and supervising staff who take care of these functions. In others, it means entering into contractual arrangements with companies providing such services. This may include developing and issuing bid statements, evaluating competitive bids, and selecting the recipients of contracts or recommending choices to the owners.

They also buy supplies and equipment; arrange for repairs or renovations; and see that local, state, and federal laws are observed. These might range from meeting fire and safety requirements to seeing that laws covering antidiscrimination and the rights of those with disabilities are met.

Managers in this area also perform various evaluation and problem-solving functions. If tenants have complaints, it is their responsibility to respond to them. These might range from problems with heating or cooling systems to dissatisfaction with custodial staff or other support services. Responses might include writing letters, memos, or E-mail messages; ordering repairs or new equipment; holding meetings with staff to discuss problems and plan corrective measures; or revising budgets to take into account funding needs for unplanned but needed improvements.

As an example of a typical role in this field, consider a large apartment complex located near a university. Primarily catering to students, the complex requires day-to-day oversight by a property management professional.

This manager, who lives in one of the apartments herself as a condition of employment, handles a wide range of duties including tenant relations, marketing, safety oversight, risk management, and asset preservation. When students, parents, or others inquire about the apartments, she provides basic information about apartment size and other features, rental rates, deposits, utilities, lease terms, and availability of units. To those who come on site, she shows empty apartments and answers questions, and then handles lease agreements for those who choose to move into the complex.

As a daily part of her job, the manager supervises a staff of five workers, evaluates the property's condition, and maintains an aggressive customer service program. She makes sure that problems ranging from stopped-up drains to disputes over parking are handled. She also keeps track of finances, makes sure all local housing regulations are met, and reports regularly to the owners on the property's condition.

Some property managers do not work on-site. Instead, they operate from corporate offices or other locations, performing work that is not that different from that of on-site personnel, but often with the added dimension of being responsible for a number of properties. In addition, they may supervise on-site managers or other personnel.

Typically, managers in this role serve in a liaison capacity between the property owner and on-site manager. Their duties may include using advertising or other methods to market vacant space to prospective tenants. They also may establish rental rates.

Real Estate Asset Managers

Property managers known as real estate asset managers serve as agents and advisers for property owners. Their duties include acting on behalf of businesses and investors to plan and direct the purchase, development, and disposition of real estate. Rather than attention to the daily operations of the properties, the focus of their work tends to be on long-term financial planning.

For most such positions, a major role is identifying potential property acquisitions. In carrying out this function, asset managers consider various factors including population trends, zoning regulations, traffic volume, taxes, and patterns in development or use of adjacent and nearby properties. When a potential property has been identified, they maintain communication with its owners or their agents, negotiate contracts for leasing or purchasing property, and follow through on sale or lease transactions.

For existing properties, real estate asset managers play an oversight role regarding profitability and other factors. For example, they review their company's real estate holdings on a regular basis and evaluate the strengths and weaknesses they offer. When they reach an assessment that a property is no longer commercially attractive, they may take steps to remove it from their company's holdings. This sometimes involves terminating a lease or negotiating the sale of the property in question.

Community Association Managers

Property managers designated as community association managers serve home-owner and condominium associations. Employed by these groups in arrangements where they normally report to a board of directors, they provide oversight and day-to-day management of property owned by members of the association. For example, a group of home owners in a suburban area might band together and form an association to protect mutual interests: making sure each home owner maintains certain standards in property care, guarding against theft or other crimes, and providing services of benefit to all those who live within the area covered by the agreement they have all signed as members of the organization.

According to the Community Associations Institute, these kinds of planned communities began to develop at the end of the nineteenth century, as growth in cities and suburbs prompted the creation of carefully designed practices for housing development. Today, approximately 47 million Americans live within community associations, according to the institute, with more than 231,000 community associations now operating. As new homes are built in or near metropolitan areas, increasing numbers fall within community associations.

For large home-owner associations, managers may be involved in providing services related to the needs of hundreds or even thousands of individual homes. Their duties might range from managing the group's budget and financial records to seeing that landscaping, parking, and street maintenance are taken care of properly. They might also oversee operation of community centers, golf courses, swimming pools, playgrounds, or other facilities used by home owners and their families, as well as resolve disputes among neighbors, meet regularly with a board of directors maintained by the association, and solve environmental or legal problems.

According to the Community Associations Institute, professionals in this area should be proficient at dealing with tasks involving management or knowledge of human resources, contracting, accounting, insurance, physical plant maintenance, government relations, board management, construction, and law and other matters.

A list of typical duties compiled by the institute includes the following:

- Providing administrative, operational, and managerial advice to association boards and residents
- Directing association personnel
- Directing the enforcement of community association rules and restrictions
- Developing association budgets and financial reports
- Assisting board members in the selection of contractors and insurance providers
- Overseeing and authorizing payment for community association services
- Performing site inspections

Farm Managers

A specialty related to more general property management is that of farm management. While partially addressed elsewhere in this book, this specialty deserves mention within the overall area of property management. It is the job of farm managers to see that farms provide the maximum possible returns for their owners. According to the American Society of Farm Managers and Rural Appraisers (ASFMRA), such returns may include financial gains produced from crops or livestock, rent income, and capital gains realized when land increases in value.

Farm managers fill a number of roles. In some cases, they help farmers or other interested parties locate land for farming purposes. In working with functioning farms, they oversee daily operations on behalf of the property owners. As pointed out by the ASFMRA, in this capacity they may perform functions such as keeping records, supervising or performing farm maintenance, handling funds, selecting and dealing with tenants, marketing crops or livestock, and purchasing supplies such as seed, pesticides, and fertilizer.

The ASFMRA is a good source of additional information about this area. In addition, the association provides a variety of services for members. Along with farm managers, this organization serves rural appraisers, review appraisers, and agricultural consultants. It provides a wide range of training opportunities and offers special designations including that of Accredited Farm Manager, and various levels of membership including professional, candidate, student, academic, affiliate, associate, retired, honorary, dual, and inactive levels.

Services include professional meetings, publications ranging from newsletters to an association journal, professional development and continuing education opportunities, and representation in government issues.

For more information, contact:

American Society of Farm Managers and Rural Appraisers
950 South Cherry Street, Suite 508
Denver, CO 80246-2664
303-758-3513
asfmra.org

Government Property Managers

While the typical position in property management may be found in the private sector, some jobs can also be found in government agencies. The federal government, state governments, and other government entities own substantial amounts of property. To manage such assets, they employ property management specialists at various levels.

For example, the U.S. Department of Agriculture operates a property management program through its Property Management Division. This unit develops, implements, monitors, and provides department-wide policies, procedures, and regulations for the management of personal and real property.

While the department's personal property consists largely of aircraft and motor vehicles and thus falls outside of the domain of real estate, its real property consists of large amounts of real estate. In fact, the U.S. Department of Agriculture is the second-largest landholder in the federal government. It owns more than 190 million acres of land and occupies more than 50 million square feet of building space, which it owns or leases.

THE PEOPLE WITH WHOM PROPERTY MANAGERS WORK

On an everyday basis, those employed in this field may encounter a variety of clients, fellow employees, and others. Of course, a major factor is the type of organization for which one works.

According to the Institute of Real Estate Management (IREM), typical employers of property or real estate managers include the following:

- Development companies, where staff manage company-owned properties and may take care of tasks from marketing to renovating properties
- Full-service real estate companies, where property management may be one of several functions handled by the firm
- Property management firms, which specialize in fee-based real estate management services for property owners
- Real estate investment trusts, in which groups of investors pool funds used to purchase a portfolio of properties, and then asset managers help assure that they maintain profit levels
- Commercial banks, which may own investment properties as a means of diversifying their holdings or hold real estate in trust, and

thus employ managers to take care of these properties or to manage properties obtained though foreclosures

- Corporations, which often employ real estate managers to oversee properties owned for conducting business
- Government agencies, which employ managers for government housing programs as well as maintenance of government-owned real estate
- Insurance companies, which may own real estate as a part of their investment programs
- Other property owners and users including mortgage brokerage companies, colleges and universities, the military, and nonprofit organizations

Within these various types of settings, property managers interact with a variety of people. In an apartment complex, they may deal with families, couples, or individual tenants. With a mall or shopping center, they work closely with owners, managers, and employees of retail establishments, as well as with the general public. In business settings, they may deal more with management personnel.

Property managers also communicate frequently with equipment service personnel, representatives of utility companies, sales reps, and others. They may also supervise clerical staff, maintenance workers, or other staff.

THE SETTINGS IN WHICH PROPERTY MANAGERS WORK

According to the IREM, the following types of property may need the services of a property or real estate manager:

- Apartments
- Cooperatives and condominiums
- Community and home-owners' associations
- Facilities or corporately owned properties
- Federally assisted housing
- Industrial properties
- Malls and outlet centers

- Mobile home parks
- Office buildings
- Public housing
- Rental homes for single families
- Retail stores
- Shopping centers
- University facilities

Within these various settings, property managers generally work in comfortable office environments. In many cases, they share office space with only a few workers, since a large number of property management firms are small, and even bigger firms may have branch offices or managers may be placed in on-site offices. In instances where the employer is a larger company, such as with some firms managing commercial properties, the office environment may be more representative of a corporate environment. Regardless of office size, managers in this field tend to experience the normal pluses of office work such as comfortable furniture and a generally pleasant environment.

At the same time, a substantial part of the work of property managers may take place outside their offices as they provide the oversight needed for properties being managed. For off-site managers, this may include frequent trips by car or other means to inspect properties, meet with people who work or live there, or take care of other matters related to caring properly for the property involved. For on-site managers, the job may entail any number of visits to facilities. For example, an apartment manager might go to individual apartments to respond to residents' complaints, meet with residents, or carry out other duties. Or a commercial property manager might walk or drive to different sites within a complex to deal with matters ranging from a problem with the heating and cooling system to looking over a newly seeded lawn to see if the grass is coming in as anticipated.

In addition, professionals in this field may have demanding requirements as far as working hours are concerned. It is not unusual for property managers to be on an "on call" status, necessitating their being available to take phone calls and deal with problems during nights or weekends. Depending on the position, they might also be expected to put in routine office hours outside the scope of the traditional forty-hour workweek.

TRAINING AND OTHER QUALIFICATIONS

Although set requirements do not exist, most employers prefer to hire college graduates in property management positions. A bachelor's degree in business administration, marketing, real estate, accounting, or a related field can be a good beginning point. Previous experience working in an office or management role can also be helpful. Computer capabilities, good communications skills, and evidence of the ability to work well independently are also valuable.

Some property managers obtain professional certifications that testify to their training and competency. For example, those involved in managing community associations may seek the following certifications:

- Certified Manager of Community Associations (CMCA)
- Association Management Specialist
- Professional Community Association Manager

Each of these designations attests to a specified level of knowledge and experience. The certification programs for these designations are administered by the National Board of Certification for Community Association Managers, which is affiliated with the Community Associations Institute and follows standards established by the National Commission for Certifying Agencies. It offers examinations that test knowledge of community association management principles.

To prepare for the national certification examination, current or prospective property managers first complete a course entitled Essentials of Community Association Management. After successfully completing this course and the national exam, they earn the CMCA credential.

After earning certification, those who earn this designation agree to follow specific standards of professional conduct in areas such as complying with federal, state, and local laws; following association and client governing documents and procedures; disclosing conflicts of interest; and other standards. To keep their certification, holders of the CMCA designation complete sixteen hours of continuing education every two years, which may consist of completing courses, reading publications, or completing self-directed studies.

The Society of Industrial and Office Realtors offers a special certification for those who qualify. The SIOR (Specialist, Industrial and Office Real Estate) designation is awarded to professionals who demonstrate a high level of knowledge in this field. It may be earned in one of five specialist categories: Advisory Services Specialist; Industrial Specialist; Industrial and Office (Dual) Specialist; Office Specialist; or Sales Management Specialist.

To qualify, brokers must have at least five years of industrial or office real estate experience and be actively engaged as an industrial or office real estate broker or salesperson, or have educational attainments to offset part of the experience requirement. They must also maintain a specified amount of sales per year and a minimum number of transactions or square footage, uphold high ethical standards of practice, and meet certain educational requirements.

For more details, contact the society at:

Society of Industrial and Office Realtors
700 Eleventh Street NW, Suite 510
Washington, DC 20001-4511
202-737-1150
sior.com

ADVANCEMENT POSSIBILITIES

Property managers may advance in their careers in several ways. One path is to start out as an assistant manager and then, after gaining experience and job skills, advance to the position of manager within the same organization. With additional experience and positive job performance, further advancement may be possible to middle or upper-level management positions, such as director of a branch office or unit within a large company, or eventually top-level positions such as vice president or even president of the company.

Another possible career path is to develop credentials and experience in one property management position, and then move to a different position with a different company.

Experienced property managers might also move to other related fields such as business management; town, county, or city administration; facilities management; health services administration; hotel management; or restaurant and food service management. They might also become real estate agents or brokers or take other positions in the real estate area.

Salaries earned by persons employed in this field vary substantially depending on factors such as experience, geographic location, and type of employer. According to the U.S. Department of Labor, about half of those employed as property, real estate, or community association managers earn salaries above $30,000 a year, and half earn salaries below this amount. The majority earn salaries between $21,000 and $43,000 a year. Some earn higher amounts, with the top 10 percent earning more than $74,500 a year.

According to the IREM, cash compensation (consisting of an employee's base salary and incentive bonuses) may be affected by a number of factors. These include previous job experience, geographic location, educational background, certifications or designations related to the real estate management industry, job level and type of responsibilities, and the industry sector or function in which a given position falls.

Once these and other relevant factors are determined, those employed as property or real estate managers can expect to earn base starting salaries as follows, according to the National Real Estate Compensation Survey compiled by CE & Associates, Inc., and reported by the IREM:

Bachelor's degree graduates	$32,000 to $46,000
Master's degree graduates	$37,000 to $55,000

In addition, managers in this field typically enjoy the potential to receive incentive bonuses, generally ranging from 5 to 15 percent of base pay. These figures reflect the norm for starting salaries; experienced managers can earn significantly higher incomes. Naturally, the higher range of salaries, both for newcomers and those experienced in the field, can be expected in metropolitan areas where the cost of living is higher than in less populated areas, or in areas where there is greater competition for qualified employees.

In addition to base salaries and incentive payments, property managers also tend to earn solid fringe benefits such as health insurance, 401(k) or other retirement programs, vacation and holiday pay, and educational assistance. Some also have the opportunity to earn stock in the company for which they are employed. Also, some property managers (typically those involved in on-site management) may receive housing allowances.

ADDITIONAL SOURCES OF INFORMATION

The following organizations offer further information on careers in property management.

Community Associations Institute

An organization of interest to many in the general area of property management is the Community Associations Institute, an association that provides education and resources to residential condominium, cooperative, and home-owner associations and related professionals and service providers. The institute offers a variety of seminars, workshops, conferences, and educational programs, some designed to lead to professional designations for those working in the field. It publishes books, guides, magazines, and specialized newsletters on community association finance, law, and management. The organization also advocates community association interests before legislative and regulatory bodies, conducts research, acts as a clearinghouse for information related to creating and managing community associations, provides networking opportunities, and offers insurance programs and other benefits.

For more information, contact:

Community Associations Institute
225 Reinekers Lane, Suite 300
Alexandria, VA 22314
703-548-8600

National Association of Residential Property Managers

Recognizing that more than one in ten single-family dwellings across the nation are non–owner occupied, the National Association of Residential Property Managers (NARPM) is a trade organization serving the increasing number of persons serving as residential property managers. It provides referrals, marketing support, networking opportunities, and other services for members including various publications, a membership directory, website, and local chapter memberships. The association fosters education through an annual convention and concurrent trade show, a midyear conference, state conferences, property management courses, seminars, and roundtable workshops.

The association also offers certification programs leading to the designation of Professional Property Manager (PPM), which is awarded to licensed real estate agents who complete the required NARPM course work, have hands-on experience in the management of residential property, and have provided service to the association; and the designation of Master Property Manager, which is awarded to members who have achieved the PPM designation and have completed additional requirements for education and experience.

For more information, contact:

National Association of Residential Property Managers
P.O. Box 140647
Austin, TX 78714-0647
800-782-3452
narpm.org

National Association of Housing and Redevelopment Officials

The National Association of Housing and Redevelopment Officials is a leading housing and community development advocate, serving members who administer government housing programs. It has nearly six thousand members who administer more than 1.3 million units of public housing. The association provides a variety of seminars, certification, and technical services programs. It offers three certification designations, software, audio seminars, on-site seminars, and other programs and services.

For more information, contact:

National Association of Housing and Redevelopment Officials
630 Eye Street NW
Washington, DC 20001
877-866-2476 (toll-free) or 202-289-3500

CoreNet Global

An organization of interest to those concerned with corporate real estate is CoreNet Global, which serves business leaders engaged in the strategic management of real estate for major corporations. Typical members are professionals who manage highly valuable real estate assets for companies whose primary business is not real estate.

Members include those who have real estate (or real estate–related) responsibilities in workplace or infrastructure management for public, private, or government organizations; service provider members in professions and related real estate functions that serve the needs of corporate real estate executives; real estate educators; students; and journalists.

Among other services, the organization provides comprehensive career services for those who are seeking employment in the corporate real estate profession.

For more details, contact:

CoreNet Global
440 Columbia Drive, Suite 100
West Palm Beach, FL 33409
800-726-8111
nacore.com

C H A P T E R

7

LAND DEVELOPMENT

An especially challenging area within the overall real estate world is land development. This involves taking land and turning it into some type of profitable development. For example, an unused section of woods might be cleared, subdivided, and transformed into a housing development. Or a pasture might be turned into the site for an industrial park or a warehouse converted to an office building.

THE NATURE OF THE WORK

Land developers undertake various types of projects in which real estate is improved. They perform functions such as selecting sites for development, developing plans for layout, making cost estimates, and coordinating efforts to obtain financing. They may also oversee construction of buildings, identify prospective buyers, and market properties once they have been developed.

For example, one type of land development is creating a business park or industrial park, where a community tries to promote economic development by encouraging businesses to locate operations at a setting designed specifically for business development. Such an enterprise entails a great deal of planning and development, including conducting feasibility studies, arranging for financing, planning for preliminary site development, designing plans for construction of new buildings or renovation of existing ones, and mapping out diverse strategies to attract tenants or buyers of business properties.

Those who deal with land development face a variety of issues and tasks. For example, they must obtain a variety of permits from town, county, or state government agencies. They must arrange for water, electricity, or other utilities. Sometimes, land developers include road or street construction as a part of their plans.

Personnel employed in land development may specialize in any of a number of areas. They might hold positions such as project engineer, surveyor, project manager, landscape architect, or planner. Others may focus on executive management, sales, or financial administration.

Typical functions undertaken in land development may include:

- Conducting feasibility studies
- Analyzing environmental impact
- Addressing zoning concerns
- Developing water and sewer systems
- Conducting boundary surveys
- Planning for telecommunications needs
- Developing and implementing landscaping plans
- Planning for property access

According to the National Association of Industrial and Office Properties, developers are among the most entrepreneurial of real estate professionals. Not only do they acquire land, but they sometimes prepare it for development and may also oversee the construction process.

Most developers specialize in either residential or commercial development. Within these areas, they may specialize to a further degree according to property size and type.

Some firms in this area are quite large, and may take on projects on a regional, national, or international basis. With larger companies, a number of specialists are often employed. Developers may be affiliated as subcontracting consultants, specializing in project management, financing, or other areas.

THE PEOPLE WITH WHOM LAND DEVELOPERS WORK

Land developers work with a wide range of people. Any one project can involve contact with a diverse array of individuals and organizations. Some of the people involved might be individuals, families, or companies owning property to be purchased or sold; real estate agents or brokers; appraisers or building inspectors; potential investors; loan officers or other bank personnel; government officials; contractors; planning officials; marketing specialists; accountants; lawyers; or others.

Within their own companies, developers also interact routinely with clerical staff, other managers, and the various people required to run any business. Through professional organizations and other affiliations, as well as through business deals, they also work with other land developers and those with related interests.

All told, the diversity in the people with whom land developers work is one of the most attractive features of this occupation. Those with good "people skills," along with the necessary technical ability, may flourish in this area.

THE SETTINGS IN WHICH LAND DEVELOPERS WORK

Those employed in land development work for a variety of employers. Perhaps most typical is a position in a large real estate company that either specializes in land development or includes it as a major part of its operations. The following overview of several actual companies illustrates some of the employment situations that may be found in land development.

Genesis Land Development

Headquartered in Calgary, Alberta, Canada's Genesis Land Development Corporation is a publicly trading land development company. It also maintains regional offices in Edmonton and Vancouver. The company has acquired more than 4,400 acres of prime development lands since its founding in 1992, and plans to convert this land into more than eighteen thousand dwelling sites.

Genesis has been involved in a number of land development projects. Recent initiatives have included acquisition of acreage for future commercial and light industrial development, and a joint shopping center project with another company.

McMillin Land Development

Located in southern California, McMillin Land Development has developed a number of master-planned communities including Rancho del Rey in Chula Vista, Scripps Ranch Villages in San Diego, and Temeku Hills Golf and Country Club in Temecula.

Among other projects, the company has developed multifaceted communities that include not just homes but also schools, parks and other recreation facilities, churches, and child-care centers. A goal of McMillin Land Development has been to create communities that offer a wide range of experiences and that appeal to people from diverse backgrounds.

Centex Corporation

Founded in Dallas, Texas, in 1950, Centex Corporation is a huge company providing services in home building, home services, financial services, contracting and construction services, construction products, and investment real estate. The company's investment real estate group includes Centex Development Company, which obtains, develops, and sells land for a variety of purposes and develops facilities for business and other uses.

An example of its many successful projects is Vista Ridge Business Park in Lewisville and Coppell, Texas. This thousand-acre master-planned development includes homes, offices, retail establishments, and other features. Its development included construction of roadways, a four-mile levee system, lakes, a public amphitheater, trails, and a sports complex.

Another example is Southpointe in Plantation, Florida, a 127-acre business park. Its development included excavation of a seventeen-acre retention lake and an intensive effort to raise the level of the site and build a landscape buffer along adjoining roads. The site offers nearly one million square feet of office space and over one hundred hotel rooms, and also holds room for further development.

In these and other companies, land developers work in environments not unlike those of other real estate professionals.

TRAINING AND OTHER QUALIFICATIONS

With the diversity found in the general area of real estate development, there is no single set of requirements regarding educational background or qualifications. For those involved in selling any type of land, the same kind of background one would expect of an agent or broker (see earlier chapters) can be a good start. For those emphasizing construction, a background in engineering, architecture, hands-on construction, or other areas can be helpful. Within specialized areas, training in marketing, management, law, environmental engineering, or other areas can be applicable.

For some positions, a bachelor's degree in business or an M.B.A. (master of business administration) degree can be a good source of all-around preparation for success. Many professionals in this general area combine different types of training (for instance, a bachelor's in a construction-related field and a master's in business). Some also use their own experience as contractors, investors in construction projects, or managers as an entry into the field.

In addition, some professionals in this area seek certification through professional associations. For example, the BCCR certification (for Board Certified in Corporate Real Estate) is available by meeting certain standards established by the International Development Research Council (IDRC).

ADVANCEMENT POSSIBILITIES

Many real estate developers begin their careers as agents or brokers, and then as they gain experience, begin to focus on land development. Others start out as contractors or professionals in the mortgage or finance area.

Persons working in land development may advance in their careers in any number of ways. One approach is to start their own development firm, or to expand an existing business specializing in some aspect of land development. Potentially, this can be a path that is very rewarding financially, and one measure of advancement can be increased earnings due to successful development projects. Some developers who become very successful might begin to act primarily as investors themselves rather than as managers of the process, if they elect this option.

Another approach is to advance within the corporate world. This path involves working within a company dealing in development projects, and then moving up to higher-level positions. For those successful in such roles, options may include continuing with one company or moving to another employer when the right opportunity arises.

In many positions, a key to advancement is continued training and enhancement of one's personal capabilities for dealing with the challenges of the job at hand. Those who read widely in their fields, attend professional development conferences or classes, participate in professional associations, and network with others tend to strengthen their chances for advancement to a significant degree.

ADDITIONAL SOURCES OF INFORMATION

The organizations described in the following sections offer further information on careers in land development.

Realtors Land Institute

An affiliate of the National Association of Realtors, the Realtors Land Institute focuses on various types of land brokerage transactions including farms and ranches, undeveloped tracts of land, transitional and development land, subdivision and wholesaling of lots, and site selection and assemblage of land parcels. It supports the needs and interests of real estate professionals in activities related to land brokerage, agribusiness, and other areas related to land development.

Of special note are the organization's land education program and professional certification program, which allows those who are qualified to earn the Accredited Land Consultant (ALC) designation.

Roles fulfilled by this organization include:

- Identifying members as land specialists within the real estate profession
- Developing and maintaining professional standards of practice
- Fostering professional expertise through educational activities
- Awarding the professional designation of ALC to members who have met rigid educational and experience requirements
- Formulating recommendations for public policy affecting land use
- Advocating the wise use of land and the reasonable rights and privileges of private ownership
- Enhancing members' business activities through marketing efforts

For more information, contact:

Realtors Land Institute
430 North Michigan Avenue
Chicago, IL 60611
800-441-LAND
rliland.com

National Association of Home Builders

The National Association of Home Builders, which operates as a federation of more than eight hundred state and local builders associations, has more than two hundred thousand members including home builders, remodelers, mortgage industry professionals, and providers of building products and services. The organization promotes the building industry and works to maintain housing as a national priority.

The association provides a variety of services to members. It also operates a research center that develops, tests, and evaluates new materials, methods, standards, and equipment used in the building and housing areas.

The group's educational arm, the Home Builders Institute, offers a variety of educational and job training programs.

For more information, contact:

National Association of Home Builders
1201 Fifteenth Street NW
Washington, DC 20005-2800
800-368-5242, ext. 0, or 202-266-8200
nahb.com

International Development Research Council

The International Development Research Council (IDRC) serves the professional interests of managers of corporate assets including corporate real estate, facilities, information technology, human resources, finance, and other support units. It provides members a wealth of information on workplace and asset management including research bulletins and reports, newsletters, and other publications. Professional development opportunities include courses, conferences, seminars, and networking, as well as certification programs.

Members fall within four membership categories: active, associate, academic, and retired.

More details are available by contacting:

IDRC North America Headquarters
35 Technology Parkway, Suite 150
Norcross, GA 30092-2901
770-446-8955
idrc.org

International Council of Shopping Centers

The International Council of Shopping Centers (ICSC) is a large global trade association serving the shopping center industry. It has some thirty-nine thousand members in the United States, Canada, and other nations. Along with shopping center owners, its members include developers as well as marketing specialists, investors, lenders, retailers, and others.

The organization sponsors approximately three hundred meetings a year and provides a variety of services and products. Members benefit from publications, research data, professional development opportunities, and more.

For more details, contact ICSC's New York headquarters as follows:

International Council of Shopping Centers
1221 Avenue of the Americas
New York, NY 10020-1099
646-728-3800
icsc.org

C H A P T E R

8

URBAN AND REGIONAL PLANNING

An area closely related to real estate is that of urban and regional planning. According to the U.S. Department of Labor, urban and regional planners (also referred to as community or city planners) develop land use plans to provide for growth and revitalization of urban, suburban, and rural communities, both on a long-term and short-term basis. In the process, they assist local officials in making decisions about social, economic, and environmental problems.

A major role of planners is promoting the best use of a given community's land and resources for residential, commercial, institutional, or recreational purposes. They may also deal with related matters such as public transportation, resource development, environmental protection, traffic congestion, or infrastructure support such as the construction of public housing, government offices, correctional facilities, or school buildings. Their work may range from helping determine the best location for a new water treatment plant to planning the construction of a new school or government office building.

THE NATURE OF THE WORK

A major part of the job of urban and regional planners is evaluating existing resources in light of future needs. For example, a planner might study the condition and availability of land used for public parks and then create plans for future land acquisition or development. Another typical effort would be studying population trends and other demographic data and then projecting future needs in key areas such as housing, water and sewage, public transportation, or school construction.

Typical tasks involved in this area include writing reports, helping draft legislation, conducting surveys, attending meetings, and keeping current on information such as zoning regulations, building codes, and environmental regulations. Planners also spend significant time in communicating with builders; developers; governing boards; the general public; and city, county, state, or federal officials. In some cases, this includes making presentations before small or large groups.

Those employed in planning employ skills in organization of information, data analysis, and written and oral communications to carry out their duties. They also use computers for word processing, report preparation, data analysis, and other purposes. This may include use of computer databases, spreadsheets, and computerized geographic information systems.

The range of duties for a position in this field varies widely. Often, the size of the employing organization is a determining factor. In small organizations, planners must be able to undertake various kinds of planning, and may be the only staff member assigned to planning functions, or one of just a few. In larger organizations, planners may specialize in a single area such as economic development, urban design, environmental issues, transportation, demography, housing, or historic preservation.

Typical job titles in this field include the following:

- Assistant planning director
- Assistant planning manager
- Director of community development
- Director of planning
- Director of planning and budgeting
- Director of planning and development
- Planner
- Planner I
- Planner II
- Planning manager
- Principal planner
- Project planner

- Senior planner
- Transportation/geographic information systems planner
- Urban planner

A look at ads for job openings in this field can be revealing of the duties performed and the qualifications required.

For example, a midsize southern city recently advertised for the position of Planner II. Applicants were expected to have experience in regulations dealing with zoning, site planning, landscaping, parking, sign regulations, urban design review, and landscape architecture. Primary work would include working with members of the building and development community, government officials, and citizens. Other responsibilities included making presentations to appropriate boards and commissions, assisting in public relations efforts, and helping implement revised land use policies.

To qualify for consideration for this position, applicants were expected to have at least two years of planning experience along with a master's degree in planning or a closely related field, or additional experience if lacking a master's degree.

As another example, a northeastern planning agency serving two counties and a city advertised for a Principal Planner dealing primarily with long-range planning duties. Areas of responsibility included comprehensive planning, population and employment forecasting, neighborhood planning, consolidated plan and environmental reviews, and special planning projects. Applicants for this job were expected to demonstrate good analytical and research skills and an understanding of innovative land use planning approaches. A master's degree in urban or regional planning, geography, or a related field was required, along with at least three years of related planning experience including a minimum of one year of management experience.

An opening for the position of Planner with a southwestern city entailed a variety of duties in city planning. Duties included reviewing permit plans for compliance with development regulations; assisting in preparing project outlines, presentations, and reports; developing urban design projects; and making recommendations on planning issues. Applicants needed a bachelor's degree in a field such as planning, urban studies, landscape architecture, public administration, or a related field along with two years of relevant job experience.

THE PEOPLE WITH WHOM URBAN AND REGIONAL PLANNERS WORK

Urban and regional planners work in a multifaceted profession. In carrying out their work, they interact with a variety of other professionals. Their supervisors may be city managers, county administrators, senior planning officials, or others. On a daily basis, they may work with secretaries, clerks, other planning officers, architects, engineers, maintenance crews, government officials, or those holding any number of responsibilities. They may also interact with citizens who could be affected by proposed development projects, reporters, business leaders, members of public boards and commissions, elected officials, and others. In fact, although of course the major portion of work completed by urban and regional planners consists of conducting planning activities, communicating with others is also a major responsibility. This may consist of one-on-one discussions by telephone or in person; E-mail correspondence; meetings of small groups ranging from staff meetings to presentations before planning commissions or boards; and in some cases, large group meetings such as public forums in which citizens are invited to comment on a proposed community project. In the process of engaging in these and other types of interactions, planners enjoy a great deal of variety. Unlike some jobs (for example, a factory assembly line where a worker sees the same few workers every day), planners routinely work with a range of people.

Employers of urban and regional planners include city governments, county governments, regional planning agencies, and other entities concerned with community development. State governments and the federal government are also employers in this area. Some urban and regional planners are employed by private companies, working in areas such as public relations or research.

THE SETTINGS IN WHICH URBAN AND REGIONAL PLANNERS WORK

Urban and regional planners work in offices in a variety of environments. A typical setting would be an office located in a courthouse annex or a complex in which offices are housed for a city manager, county administrator, and others involved in local or regional government. State or federal office buildings, corporate office complexes, and other such sites also provide working environments for planners.

Actual office environments range from the simple to the elaborate. Beginning planners may share space with other workers or might be assigned to a small office or cubicle. At a minimum, office furnishings will include a computer, desk, and telephone. Experienced planners or those housed in newly constructed facilities might enjoy roomy, well-designed offices that are both attractive and comfortable.

Substantial travel is a routine part of the job for many urban and regional planners. Planners often travel within the areas their work covers, inspecting potential construction sites, structures being renovated, or other sites. They also travel to the offices of other professionals, attend professional meetings, and travel for other purposes. In the process, they may complete some of their work in cars, hotel rooms, or other locations away from their office, or working out of their homes. In the process, they may use various types of mobile devices such as cellular phones, personal digital assistants, pagers, and notebook computers.

Most planners work approximately forty hours per week, although some put in longer hours. In many cases, the job requires attending evening meetings of boards or commissions, or holding public meetings during evening or weekend hours so citizens may be informed about proposed development projects. Sometimes the pressure of completing reports or proposals also requires working extra hours.

TRAINING AND OTHER QUALIFICATIONS

Most employers prefer that potential planners hold at least a bachelor's degree in urban and regional planning or in a closely related field. A master's degree is often required. Some successful planners combine higher education and work experience (such as a bachelor's degree and related work experience) or different disciplines in their collegiate studies (such as a bachelor's degree in engineering or architecture and a master's in urban and regional planning). In addition to courses in planning itself, courses in areas such as economics, public administration, health-care administration, geographic information systems, statistics, finance, management, earth sciences, or civil engineering can be helpful.

For the maximum benefit in possible career advancement, any degree in urban or regional planning should be earned from an institution accredited by the Planning Accreditation Board, which includes representatives from the American Planning Association, the Association of Collegiate Schools of Planning, and the American Institute of Certified Planners.

In the process of earning one or more degrees in the field, students studying planning normally specialize in one or more areas of interest. Common specialty areas include transportation, land use and comprehensive planning, economic development, social planning, urban design, historic preservation, housing, and community development. Many students complete internships to gain experience while still in college, or work in part-time or summer jobs related to planning.

Planners who gain the right combination of education and experience may earn certification from the American Institute of Certified Planners (AICP), a unit of the American Planning Association. AICP certification can be valuable in seeking new positions or advancing with existing employers.

Along with the basic academic requirements, successful planners need skill in using computers, good writing and speaking skills, and strong analytical skills. As they gain experience, most planners also improve their capabilities by attending conferences, taking additional classes, or otherwise participating in professional development activities.

ADVANCEMENT POSSIBILITIES

Advancement paths for urban or regional planners vary. One possibility is to move up from an entry-level position to a more senior position within the same agency or other employing organization. In the process, this might involve taking on more diversified management roles such as supervising office workers or conducting administrative work outside the planning domain. It is not unknown for planning officers to move up the ladder to take on more broad-based roles such as assistant city manager or county administrator and then, with additional experience, assume the top job itself.

A different path is to gain experience in one organization and then pursue employment with a different agency. For instance, a planning officer employed by a small suburban county might take a position with a large city government or multicounty regional planning agency. Or a junior-level employee in a large organization might take a high-level position in a smaller agency.

Concurrent with advancement is the potential to earn higher salaries, which can be quite good in this field. Since many employers are government agencies, salaries may not equal those of many private sector jobs, but they do offer solid earning potential along with good benefits.

Here are some representative salary ranges for positions recently advertised in this field:

Planner I	$23,985–$36,100
Planner II	$40,700–$47,350
Planner	$47,000–$71,000
Director of planning, building, and zoning	$51,000–$64,000
Project planner	$36,000–$50,000
Planning supervisor	$45,000–$46,000
Principal planner	$46,000–$65,000
Planning manager	$84,000–$104,000
Director of planning	$57,000–$68,000
Director of community development	$75,800–$95,500
Director of planning and development	$46,000–$62,500

ADDITIONAL SOURCES OF INFORMATION

The organizations described in the following sections offer further information on careers in urban and regional planning.

Urban Land Institute

A helpful source of information about issues related to urban planning is the Urban Land Institute. This organization fosters respect for the land, the profession, the consumer, and the public, among other areas of regard. Approximately fifteen thousand professionals in more than fifty countries are members.

The institute was founded in 1936, during a time of suburban expansion and urban decay. Today, the organization focuses on nonpartisan research and education in the areas of urban planning, land use, and development.

The institute sponsors research, organizes forums and task forces, provides advisory services, sponsors district councils, makes awards for excellence, publishes materials on land use and development, maintains an informative website, provides workshops, sponsors a Real Estate School, holds conferences, sponsors professional meetings, and provides other benefits to members.

For more information, contact:

Urban Land Institute
1025 Thomas Jefferson Street NW, Suite 500 West
Washington, DC 20007
202-624-7000 or 800-321-5011
uli.org

American Planning Association

Another organization of note is the American Planning Association (APA), which has some thirty thousand members with an interest in urban and rural planning issues. It has forty-six regional chapters and seventeen divisions of specialized planning interests and also offers a component known as the American Institute of Certified Planners (AICP), which certifies planners who have met specific educational and experiential requirements and who have passed a special examination.

The APA maintains two primary offices. Its national headquarters in Washington, D.C., houses the AICP and the association's policy and public information departments. The organization's research, publications, conference, education, membership, and marketing departments and council programs are located in Chicago.

The APA influences legislation, advocates policy changes, and educates media and the public about the importance of planning and the role of planners in this important enterprise. It also conducts research on planning topics and sponsors publications including *Planning*, a monthly magazine, and the quarterly *Journal of the American Planning Association*. In addition, it holds conferences and offers other educational opportunities including audio conferences, manuals, training workshops, and video- and audiotapes.

For more information, contact the organization at either of the following addresses:

American Planning Association
122 South Michigan Avenue, Suite 1600
Chicago, IL 60603
planning.org

American Planning Association
1776 Massachusetts Avenue NW
Washington, DC 20036

American Real Estate and Urban Economics Association

The American Real Estate and Urban Economics Association (AREUEA) serves the interests of academic, professional, and governmental people who are concerned with urban economics and real estate issues.

The association publishes a quarterly journal, *Real Estate Economics*, and holds three conferences yearly. It also offers other programs and services including a membership directory, job postings, and professional networking opportunities.

For more information, contact:

AREUEA
P.O. Box 1148
Portage, MI 49081-1148
866-AREUEA1
areuea.org

CHAPTER 9

REAL ESTATE COUNSELING AND RESEARCH

As noted in previous chapters, real estate transactions can be quite complicated. Potential buyers, those interested in pursuing real estate acquisitions as investment vehicles, and others frequently need specialized advice. Real estate counselors meet this demand. They answer questions about all aspects of real estate. They gather facts and assess specific situations, analyze data that have been collected, and make recommendations for action. Generally, their overall goal is to help clients improve the economic value of real property holdings.

Researchers play a similar role by gathering and analyzing information about various aspects of the world of real estate.

THE NATURE OF THE WORK

According to the Counselors of Real Estate (CRE), a leading professional association serving this field, real estate counseling differs from management, appraisal, and brokerage. Real estate counseling is a process rather than a discipline. Real estate counselors perform an important role by providing advice to others who are considering decisions regarding buying or selling property or dealing with other real estate–related matters. A real estate counselor acts as an adviser to clients regarding potential decisions by assisting in evaluating options, considering the client's best interests, and developing strategies for meeting clients' goals.

The CRE provides the following definition of this process:

Real Estate Counseling is the act of providing advice or guidance to clients which significantly impacts their real estate decisions. Such advice must be rendered solely for the use of the party or parties receiving the advice and without personal bias and/or conflict of interest. Unlike management, appraisal, or brokerage, counseling is not a discipline but a process.

Persons who are designated as a CRE by this organization must demonstrate a high level of knowledge, experience, and competency. They must also show good judgment and integrity.

They serve a variety of clients including banks and other financial institutions, lawyers, insurance companies, accountants, real estate developers, government agencies, investors, and pension funds.

CREs help clients make decisions such as whether to keep or sell a property, or to rent it or take another course of action. They provide advice in areas such as marketing, property improvement, zoning, and property disposal. They may advise on financing, dealing with special problems, and other matters for making the best use of property.

THE PEOPLE WITH WHOM REAL ESTATE COUNSELORS WORK

Real estate counselors provide advice for a wide range of individuals and organizations. Those using such services include property owners, land developers, banks and other financial institutions, real estate investors, lawyers, accountants, corporations, government agencies, and nonprofit organizations.

This means that in the routine course of their work, real estate counselors encounter a wide variety of people. In fact, diversity in the people with whom they work is one of the advantages experienced professionals cite about this specialty area.

When assisting clients, real estate counselors enjoy the satisfaction of applying their expertise to the needs of others. At the same time, they sometimes experience the pressure of realizing that their advice can determine financial success for others and may have a significant impact on transactions involving large sums of money.

THE SETTINGS IN WHICH REAL ESTATE COUNSELORS WORK

Some professionals hold full-time positions as real estate counselors. Others combine this function with other roles. For example, a broker or agent might provide counseling along with other services. In either case, a great deal of knowledge about the field is required, since clients must have confidence that the counselor is capable of providing sound advice. This knowledge may be demonstrated in any number of ways, including college background, special certifications obtained through professional associations, and previous experience. The latter is particularly important, since it is through such experience that the counselor not only develops skills and knowledge, but also builds a track record that can be used in attracting clients and indicating competencies.

Work settings tend to reflect the nature of the job at hand. Typically, real estate counselors enjoy attractive, comfortable office work environments. They may spend an appreciable part of their time sitting at executive desks or computer workstations, where they complete paperwork, talk on the phone, read and write E-mail, and perform other functions. Other frequent work sites include conference rooms and boardrooms, offices of clients, and other similar locations. Their work may also involve traveling in cars, airplanes, or other modes of transportation.

Typically, real estate counselors provide their services on a fee basis. Rather than working as employees and earning a salary, or garnering commissions based on a percentage of sales, they charge a fee that is established prior to the performance of services. In some cases such fees are modest, and for those who include counseling as just a portion of their duties, the activity can be seen as valuable for making contacts and planting seeds for additional business in the future. But in some circumstances, the fees involved are quite substantial. In fact, earnings can be lucrative for those who specialize in real estate consulting.

TRAINING AND OTHER QUALIFICATIONS

There is no one path leading to a career in counseling, according to the CRE. A typical first step is earning a college degree in business, real estate, or a related field. Then, experience is gained in any of several areas of real estate such as brokerage, appraising, asset management, investment, or portfolio management. Then as experience and knowledge are gained, some real estate professionals begin to provide counseling services.

ADVANCEMENT POSSIBILITIES

Most real estate counselors start out as agents or brokers. Then after benefiting from significant experience, they use the knowledge they have gained to move into a counseling role. As previously noted, some counselors include this type of work while continuing to provide other types of real estate brokerage services. Others begin to specialize in the counseling function.

One advancement possibility is to start, continue, or expand one's own business in this specialty area. Measures of success here might include increased volume of business or a continuing track record in not only satisfying existing clients, but attracting new ones.

Another path is to move up in the corporate world. Real estate counselors might take jobs with large corporations and then advance with the company based on factors ranging from their own performance to the overall growth and success of the corporation.

Regardless of the employment setting, a special need for those working in real estate advisory roles is to develop and update knowledge about current factors affecting real estate markets and related matters. This can be done in any number of ways, but one strategy is to read widely in the field. By reading newspapers, business magazines, real estate newsletters and journals, and other materials including electronic information accessed via the Internet, professionals in this area stay informed by reading about the latest developments in the world of real estate.

Most real estate counselors also find it important to maintain professional relationships that are beneficial in sharing industry-related knowledge. These may range from informal contacts to membership in various professional organizations.

ADDITIONAL SOURCES OF INFORMATION

The following organizations offer further information on careers in real estate counseling and research.

Counselors of Real Estate

A well-regarded organization serving professionals in this field is the Counselors of Real Estate. Unlike many professional associations, membership is by invitation only. To be invited, potential members must demonstrate several qualifications including a senior position in a firm, demonstrated excellence, knowledge, integrity, and judgment, and at least ten years of experience in real estate including at least three years in counseling. Prospective members must also be members of the National Association of Realtors.

The Counselors of Real Estate provides educational programs, printed and electronic information, networking opportunities, and other services for members. Publications include a quarterly journal, *Real Estate Issues (REI)*, which focuses on practical applications and applied theory; *The Counselor*, a member newsletter; an annual directory; and various books and monographs designed for professionals.

For more information, contact:

Counselors of Real Estate
430 North Michigan Avenue
Chicago, IL 60611-4089
312-329-8427
cre.org

Real Estate Consulting Group of America

Another good source of information about this area is the Real Estate Consulting Group of America. This organization is composed of recognized experts, each of whom is a principal in a company providing real estate valuation, business valuation, research, advisory, counseling, and market analysis services.

The group's services have been used by a variety of clients including individuals, corporations, government agencies, and investors.

For more information, contact the group at recga.com.

10

REAL ESTATE LAW

As discussed in earlier chapters, buying or selling land is a highly complex process, governed by a wide range of laws designed to protect the rights of those involved. As a result, appropriately trained lawyers (also called attorneys) play a vital role in the real estate enterprise.

Some lawyers specialize in working with real estate transactions. Many others include real estate as a major area of their professional work, but do not restrict their efforts to the real estate arena. For discussion purposes here, this chapter will focus on lawyers who specialize in real estate. But many of the points made here also apply to those in more general practice who include real estate as an area in which they provide professional services.

THE NATURE OF THE WORK

Real estate lawyers act as advisers to those who are buying or selling property, or to those involved in other matters related to real estate. They help process much of the paperwork involved in land transfers or other real estate transactions. Attorneys provide counsel to clients regarding their legal rights and obligations, and may suggest specific courses of action in buying or selling property or handling related matters. In this role, they research the intent of relevant laws and judicial decisions, and then apply the law to their client's specific circumstances and needs.

Examples of matters handled by real estate lawyers include:

- Acquisition of property
- Construction projects
- Contract development
- Project development
- Real estate financing
- Sale of property
- Tax planning
- Title searching and examination

Real estate lawyers spend the majority of their time outside the courtroom. They conduct research, meet with clients, process documents, and assess the legal positions of their clients in terms of the situation at hand.

Some real estate attorneys do appear in court when the work involves disputes regarding real estate–related matters. But the popular image of an attorney presenting a passionate argument to a judge and jury does not do justice to the usual work performed by real estate lawyers. Rather, the bulk of their work takes place in what might be considered the background. Nevertheless it is important work, and lawyers who focus on this area take satisfaction in applying their knowledge of the law to the needs of companies, nonprofit organizations, and private individuals.

While some attorneys specialize entirely in real estate, others make it a segment of their practice. In both cases, further specialization is possible. For example, a real estate attorney might focus only on the needs of large corporations or of certain types of business (for example, the insurance industry or the timber industry). Or a lawyer might focus on environmental law as it applies to real estate.

THE PEOPLE WITH WHOM REAL ESTATE LAWYERS WORK

Real estate attorneys work with a great variety of people. This includes not only clients from all kinds of educational and social backgrounds, but other professionals. Within their own firms, they may work with other lawyers, paralegals or legal assistants, secretaries, or other personnel. If they are employed in a large corporation rather than a law practice, their coworkers may include a variety of managers and other office workers.

Lawyers may also represent a wide range of clients from the general population. These might include families in the process of buying a home or selling property they have inherited, small business owners seeking to sell or purchase business property, or corporate executives involved in real estate acquisitions or development projects. They also interact with other professionals involved in the real estate business including appraisers, real estate agents and brokers, mortgage loan officers, tax attorneys, and other specialists.

Many real estate attorneys also participate in professional associations. This gives them the opportunity to associate with men and women who have similar professional challenges and interests. In the process, they find continuous opportunities to share information and learn more about their profession.

Real estate attorneys spend a considerable amount of time meeting with clients and other professionals. They also depend on telephone conversations, E-mail, and other means of communicating as a routine part of their jobs.

THE SETTINGS IN WHICH REAL ESTATE LAWYERS WORK

Real estate lawyers work in a variety of settings. Much activity takes place in their own offices, where they meet with clients or others. They may also put in significant time in city or county courthouses, law libraries, or conference rooms. Lawyers may also meet in the homes or offices of clients or in the offices of other attorneys. They may also appear before courts, travel to attend professional conferences or other meetings, or work in other locations depending on the circumstances at hand.

Although real estate lawyers may appear in court, this may not constitute a significant portion of their workload. More commonly, they spend the majority of their time working in their offices or in other locations, where they complete paperwork, meet with clients, or perform other tasks involved in the detailed steps making up the typical real estate transaction.

Some real estate lawyers are employed in private law practices. In addition, many attorneys in this type of environment who do not specialize in real estate handle it as a significant portion of their civil law practice. Some real estate attorneys are employed on a full-time basis by a single client. For example, they might work for a large corporation where they provide guidance regarding the company's real estate–related investments or activities related to holding, developing, buying, or selling property. Others perform similar functions as employees of state or federal government agencies.

It is not unusual for real estate lawyers to work more than eight hours per day or forty hours per week. This is especially common for less experienced attorneys who work in private firms under the direction of more experienced lawyers. For those employed by corporations or other organizations as salaried employees, work hours may be more in line with the standard forty-hour week. Similarly, those in senior positions or who operate their own practices may have more control of their own schedules. They may choose to work what might be considered long hours, or may have less intensive schedules. This can be an advantage in considering retirement possibilities, for it may be possible to work reduced hours and enter into semiretirement at a time of the attorney's choosing.

In general, the actual work environment for real estate attorneys is a pleasant one. Most activities are conducted in comfortable offices or other indoor settings.

TRAINING AND OTHER QUALIFICATIONS

Real estate lawyers, like other attorneys, must be admitted to the bar in any states in which they practice. This means that they must pass a comprehensive written examination, and in many cases also pass a separate ethics exam.

Before taking the bar exam, most states require that an applicant earn both a bachelor's degree and a law degree from an institution accredited by the American Bar Association or designated state authorities. A few states have less stringent requirements, allowing prospective lawyers to take the bar exam after studying in a law office or taking correspondence courses.

The typical path to a career as a real estate attorney begins with completion of a bachelor's degree (which may be preceded by a two-year associate degree at a community college or may be completed entirely at a four-year college or university). This is followed by three years of law school. In some cases, students attend on a part-time basis, and may need four years or more for completion.

Although the term "prelaw" is sometimes used, there is no one track to preparing for admission to law school. Students may major in political science, history, English, economics, or other fields. Undergraduate courses in real estate would be helpful for those planning a career in real estate law, but are by no means a requirement, as the necessary competencies may be gained in law school courses. While studying as undergraduates, prospective lawyers are well advised to develop their skills in writing, reading, speaking, researching, analyzing, and computing.

Getting admitted to law school can be a challenge. Since large numbers of students would like to become lawyers, the process is competitive. Students are admitted based on factors such as grades, scores on the Law School Admission Test, and potential for success as indicated by the competitiveness of their undergraduate school, personal interviews, previous work experience, or other factors.

Those who are admitted to law school face additional challenges in mastering complex material. They tend to put in long hours studying for exams, reading about various court cases, writing papers, and performing other academic work.

During the first part of their law school experience, students tend to study basic courses in areas such as legal writing, civil procedure, constitutional law, contracts, torts, and property law. Then during their second or third year, they begin to specialize in areas of interest. They may also work in legal clinics; engage in research and writing for the school's law journal; or serve in part-time or summer clerkships in law firms, corporate legal departments, or government agencies.

Along with the educational qualifications necessary to become licensed, today's real estate lawyers must also master various types of technology to perform their varied tasks more efficiently. This includes obtaining information via Internet websites, searching electronic databases, and employing general-use software as well as that designed for application in the legal profession.

ADVANCEMENT POSSIBILITIES

The majority of real estate lawyers begin their careers in salaried positions. A typical path for a recent law school graduate is to start out as an associate under the guidance of more experienced lawyers or judges. Then after gaining several years of experience, some attorneys are admitted to partnership in their firm, while others open their own practice. Those interested in the real estate field may do this work within a firm that also handles other types of legal matters, or they may be employed in a firm focusing entirely on real estate law.

Advancement possibilities beyond this point vary. One path is simply to become more and more successful as an attorney specializing in real estate. Within an existing law firm, this might mean rising to partner status and seeing earnings increase significantly over time. Or for lawyers who open their own practice, advancement might consist of seeing the firm grow larger, bringing in more business, and possibly reaching the point where other lawyers are hired. In the corporate setting, advancement might include promotions to higher positions within the company's legal department or within the overall organization itself.

Other paths to advancement might include significant career changes. For example, an attorney with the right credentials might take a job as a law school faculty member or administrator.

ADDITIONAL SOURCES OF INFORMATION

American Bar Association
750 North Lake Shore Drive
Chicago, IL 60611
abanet.org

Law School Admission Council
P.O. Box 40
Newtown, PA 18940
lsac.org

C H A P T E R

11

MORTGAGE LOAN PROCESSING

An important function that is closely related to the real estate industry is that of making loans. Loan officers play an integral role in the process of buying and selling homes, business facilities, and other types of property.

Since most real estate is quite costly (typically valued from the tens of thousands of dollars to the millions), it is common that real estate purchases are based on loans rather than outright cash purchases. As a result, a significant demand exists for personnel who process mortgages.

As pointed out by the National Association of Industrial and Office Properties (NAIOP), mortgage lenders specialize according to loan size and property type. For single-family residences, lenders include commercial banks, savings institutions, credit unions, and mortgage companies that resell loans in the secondary mortgage market.

Loan officers tend to be paid in two different ways. Those employed by banks and savings institutions usually earn a regular salary, with bonuses sometimes available. Lending officers who work for mortgage companies, on the other hand, tend to be paid according to their productivity.

Working in this field requires specialized knowledge about matters such as credit analysis, appraisals, environmental concerns, and various government regulations. Those dealing with multifamily mortgages handle property analysis tasks relating to income and expense review, tenant review, market trends, and collateral. Lending officers in this area of the industry may be employed by banks and other savings institutions, life insurance companies, pension funds, and other employers.

Because of the knowledge required, commercial mortgage lenders generally need more business education and analytical skills than do residential lenders, according to the NAIOP, with many successful professionals holding graduate degrees. The same is true of those who work in construction lending, which involves a complex range of functions. In some cases, experienced mortgage lenders move on to roles as construction lenders.

THE NATURE OF THE WORK

For the majority of families or individuals, the way to purchase a house or other real estate is to take out a loan. In the business world, loans are also a common mechanism for purchasing property. Loan officers play an important part in this process. They assist clients in applying for loans. As a part of their work, they gather financial information about clients along with other related information, often focusing on the ability to repay the loan. Their jobs may also include seeking potential clients.

Some loan officers specialize in mortgage loans, and thus have the most direct connection to the real estate industry. Others focus on commercial or consumer loans, utilizing similar training and skills and developing the potential to work with mortgage loans if they choose to go in that direction.

It is not uncommon for loan officers to function in a sales capacity. As a part of this process, they may maintain contacts with residential or commercial real estate agencies and cultivate agents so that their firm might be considered for the loans involved when properties are bought or sold.

Much of the work performed by loan officers focuses on guiding clients through the loan application process. This might include phoning or meeting with prospective clients, explaining details about types of loans, interest rates, and credit terms, and answering questions about the loan-making process. In some cases, assistance includes helping applicants complete necessary paperwork.

Substantial work is also done in analyzing loan applications once they have been submitted. This includes verifying information in the application to make sure it is accurate and determining the client's financial status. Normally this is done first by using a computer and special software to obtain a credit history, and then gathering additional information such as proof of employment; income verification; or, in the case of corporate applicants, detailed financial statements. Loan officers then consolidate all this information into a loan file and study the results. They then decide, sometimes after consulting with other managers in their organization, whether a loan will be granted and what terms will be offered to the applicant.

Other tasks performed by loan officers include setting up repayment schedules, establishing the need for collateral (for example, using the equity in a house as security for the repayment of a second mortgage or home equity loan), and obtaining the necessary signatures and other documentation required in finalizing the loan process.

Some loan officers, typically known as loan underwriters, specialize in the process of determining a client's financial situation and ability to repay a loan. They conduct detailed financial analyses or other risk assessments and report their findings to other loan officers or managers.

Some workers in this field specialize as loan counselors or loan collection officers. When borrowers become delinquent in repaying their loans, they contact clients and help arrange for repayment. If the borrower is unable to repay they initiate collateral liquidation. In the case of a home mortgage, this means that the home is seized and sold, and the proceeds are used to repay the loan.

THE PEOPLE WITH WHOM LOAN OFFICERS WORK

One of the pluses of working in this field is the chance to interact with a variety of people. In any given day or week, loan officers work with a great variety of people. Those working in the area of home mortgages deal with people from all walks of life. Loan applicants might be first-time home buyers who have never before applied for a loan, and thus rely heavily on the help provided. Or they might be experienced home owners who require a minimal level of assistance. They might be males or females, young adults or senior citizens, single or the head of a household. Loan applicants come from various racial, ethnic, and national backgrounds. Some boast solid financial resources and a strong credit rating. Others lack such a profile, and thus offer more challenges in qualifying for loans.

Regardless of the backgrounds of applicants, loan officers spend a significant amount of time communicating with them. Through phone conversations, face-to-face meetings, and other means, they have frequent conversations and other communications with clients.

In addition to dealing with clients, loan officers interact routinely with other personnel. These include other loan officers, supervisors, and clerical workers. In addition, other contacts may include real estate agents or brokers, business executives, or other managers.

To some extent, the range of people with whom loan officers work is determined by the type of organization in which they are employed. According to the U.S. Department of Labor, the industries employing the largest numbers of loan officers are commercial banks, savings institutions, mortgage banks and brokers, personal credit institutions, and credit unions. Within such organizations, they may work with other loan officers, executive managers, secretaries, receptionists, customer service representatives, underwriters, or other personnel.

According to the Mortgage Bankers Association of America, mortgage bankers are the leading group of home mortgage lenders, followed by commercial banks, and then savings and loans. Of those home loans made by mortgage bankers, about 75 percent are conventional loans, with Federal Housing Administration (FHA) loans and Veterans Administration (VA) loans representing about 25 percent of the total.

THE SETTINGS IN WHICH LOAN OFFICERS WORK

Most loan officers work in offices in banks or other financial institutions. This means that they experience the usual comforts of an office environment and are not required to perform work of a challenging physical nature. Office environments vary widely. Some loan officers work in a small cubicle with little more than a desk, telephone, and computer. Others enjoy roomy surroundings with comfortable and attractive furnishings.

For many loan officers, substantial travel is a routine part of the job. They may travel to the homes or offices of clients, working out of their home or car and using portable equipment such as laptop computers, cellular phones, personal digital assistants, pagers, and fax machines to maintain communications with loan applicants and their home offices. For loans involving commercial real estate or other types of business loans, travel from one city or state to another may also be required.

Loan officers might also travel to attend conferences, classes, or other professional development opportunities.

For some loan officers, a forty-hour workweek is the norm. For others, additional work during evenings and weekends is not unusual. Since many mortgage loan officers may take on as many clients as their time allows, working extra hours is routine. When mortgage interest rates dip to lower levels, which happens periodically depending on economic conditions, loan officers who deal with such loans may be especially busy.

TRAINING AND OTHER QUALIFICATIONS

Although there is no hard-and-fast set of requirements in this field, most employers prefer that potential loan officers hold a bachelor's degree in business administration, finance, economics, or another business-related field. Skills in using computers are also required, as are skills in customer relations. Those with previous experience in sales may have an advantage over other applicants, especially for mortgage loan officers.

Some workers who do not have a college degree may advance to loan positions through on-the-job training and experience. For example, bank tellers or customer service reps who perform well in their jobs may be promoted to positions as loan officers.

In addition to the program-based business courses available at most colleges and universities, those interested in careers as loan officers may take advantage of educational opportunities offered by professional associations. For example, the American Institute of Banking (AIB), an affiliate of the American Bankers Association, offers courses both for experienced loan officers and those interested in breaking into this field. Many of this organization's courses are offered by colleges and universities through joint agreements with the AIB, while others may be taken through a distance-learning format.

Another provider of classes related to real estate lending is the Mortgage Bankers Association. Through its School of Mortgage Banking, this organization provides classes both through traditional classroom formats and through Web-based alternative approaches. Some classes are designed for experienced loan officers as continuing education opportunities, while others provide helpful background for persons interested in becoming loan officers.

In addition to the necessary training or experience, loan officers should exhibit certain basic traits. They need solid communication skills (both oral and written) and should also have a flair for working with people. Good math skills and comfort in working with numbers are also helpful.

ADVANCEMENT POSSIBILITIES

Several advancement paths are possible for loan officers. One approach is to move up from a small office or branch to a larger operation within the same organization. Another is to take on a management position. Typically, a first move in this direction would involve supervising clerical workers or other loan officers. Additional advancement as a manager might involve diversifying and taking on more broad-based administrative responsibilities. Typically, additional education or experience outside the lending area would be needed for continued advancement into the executive management area.

Another possibility is to use the experience gained in one organization as a springboard to a position with a different company. For example, a loan officer employed by a small private mortgage firm might take a position with a larger company. In addition to paying a higher salary, such a job might offer more options in terms of future advancement within the organization.

Still another possibility is to use the business skills and personal contacts gained as a loan officer in starting a small business. Some loan officers have gone on to establish their own third-party home mortgage brokerage companies or develop other types of small businesses.

ADDITIONAL SOURCE OF INFORMATION

The Mortgage Bankers Association of America (MBA), with headquarters in Washington, D.C., has more than three thousand members involved in real estate finance. Member institutions include mortgage companies, mortgage brokers, commercial banks, credit unions, savings and loan associations, savings banks, and life insurance companies.

Members of this association provide mortgages to those buying homes as well as to commercial enterprises. Many of the clients are low-income or middle-income borrowers seeking loans backed by the FHA or VA.

This association provides a variety of services to members, including representing their interests to Congress and regulatory agencies. The MBA is also a good source of statistics about this industry.

For more information, contact:

Mortgage Bankers Association of America
1919 Pennsylvania Avenue NW
Washington, DC 20006-3438
mbaa.org

12

CONSTRUCTION AND BUILDING INSPECTION

A major issue in the real estate industry is safety. When new homes, commercial buildings, or other structures are constructed, various laws require that they be built safely. When existing structures are modified, they must often be inspected for the same reasons.

Similarly, the transfer of ownership of a house or other structure also involves an inspection process. Typically, a prospective buyer wants to make sure that the property in question is free of any defects that might pose a danger or diminish its value. Home inspectors evaluate residential property and compile reports about its condition.

The need for such services provides for a major employment category related to the real estate industry. Home inspectors and other types of building inspectors perform important contributions in this area.

THE NATURE OF THE WORK

According to the U.S. Department of Labor, construction and building inspectors "examine the construction, alteration, or repair of buildings, highways and streets, sewer and water systems, dams, bridges, and other structures to ensure compliance with building codes and ordinances, zoning regulations, and contract specifications." The purpose of compliance is to ensure the health and safety of the general public.

In the residential real estate industry, home inspectors play a major role. They conduct detailed inspections of newly built homes as well as those that have been previously owned. Inspectors evaluate a home's structural quality as well as features such as heating or cooling systems, roofing, electrical systems, and plumbing.

Often, families or other prospective home buyers employ home inspectors before they make an offer to buy, or they make the agreement to purchase contingent on receiving a favorable report from a home inspector.

Other types of inspectors deal with various specialty areas. In many cases, they deal with facilities other than homes such as commercial buildings, industrial sites, or specific components within buildings.

For example, plumbing inspectors deal with plumbing systems. They may inspect plumbing fixtures and traps, water supply and distribution systems, or waste disposal systems. Electrical inspectors, on the other hand, focus on electrical systems and equipment to make sure they function properly and that all electrical codes and standards are followed. Inspectors in this area examine wiring, lighting, motors, and other electrical equipment. This can include generating equipment, security systems, or wiring for heating and cooling systems.

Other inspectors focus on elevators and other lifting and conveying devices; public works such as highways, bridges, dams, or water and sewage systems; or mechanical equipment such as commercial kitchen appliances or heating and air-conditioning equipment.

The work of inspectors varies according to the type of structures or components being examined. For construction projects, typical tasks include first making a preliminary inspection during the first part of the project, and later making one or more follow-up inspections to see that relevant regulations are followed. During this process, a major focus is ensuring compliance with safety regulations along with structural considerations. Those serving as specification inspectors focus on design specifications. Rather than represent the interests of the general public, they serve the needs of the owners of the property or of financial institutions or insurance companies.

For existing structures, such as private homes being inspected prior to a sale, the emphasis is not just on safety, but also on identifying any problems that might make the home less valuable than the asking price, or that might need improvement or correction. This process includes describing the condition of the property in a report that is included with the legal papers filed during the change of ownership.

The actual work conducted when inspecting homes, commercial properties, or equipment requires thoroughness and attention to detail. In many cases, visual inspection provides the majority of information. In addition, inspectors may take photographs or use devices such as survey instruments, tape measures, or metering devices. They may also operate notebook computers or other electronic devices to record information while in the field.

THE PEOPLE WITH WHOM BUILDING AND CONSTRUCTION INSPECTORS WORK

Building and construction inspectors also experience a high level of variety in terms of contact with people. They may encounter home owners from a variety of backgrounds as well as other inspectors, real estate agents, contractors, engineers, government officials, or others. At the same time, they may also put in significant time working by themselves. While in very large construction projects a team of inspectors may be involved, the typical inspection job is performed by one individual working alone.

More than half of all construction and building inspectors work for local and state governments. City and county building departments are frequent employers. In big cities or counties, the size of inspection staffs may be quite large.

Other employers include engineering firms, architectural services companies, and other types of companies.

THE SETTINGS IN WHICH BUILDING AND CONSTRUCTION INSPECTORS WORK

An advantage of a career in this field is that there is great variety in daily work environments. Unlike many occupations that involve showing up at the same work site day after day, building inspectors move about extensively as they visit the sites they are inspecting. In the process, they experience a tremendous variety in work surroundings.

In many cases, inspection sites are dirty and cluttered, necessitating the use of safety equipment such as steel-toed shoes, hard hats, or gloves. Climbing or crawling within tight spaces may be required, and care must be taken when working around debris, tools, and construction materials.

Construction and building inspectors also spend some time in offices. Whether this entails a home-based office or company-based facilities, their work includes functions such as scheduling inspections; writing reports; reviewing blueprints; or answering letters, telephone calls, or E-mail messages. In the process, they may work with notebook or desktop computers, fax machines, computer printers, and other types of office equipment.

Significant time may also be spent in cars, trucks, or other forms of transportation as inspectors move from their homes or offices to each inspection site.

TRAINING AND OTHER QUALIFICATIONS

Requirements vary in terms of the education and training necessary to succeed in this field. First of all, building and construction inspectors need familiarity with the construction process. This may be gained through work experience as a carpenter, plumber, electrician, or other craftsperson, or as another type of worker in this field.

In addition, some type of formal education related to the field is desirable. Many inspectors earn a certificate or degree in building inspection technology from a community or technical college, where they complete courses in areas such as fundamentals of building inspection, blueprint reading, drafting, construction technology, algebra, geometry, business writing, and computer use.

Other requirements include a valid driver's license, the ability to walk and climb as needed, and in some cases, successful completion of a civil service exam. Also important is the completion of continuing education courses or other educational opportunities to stay current in the field. These might consist of in-house training provided by employers, college courses or noncredit seminars, correspondence or Internet-based courses, and state-sponsored training seminars and conferences, or seminars sponsored by professional associations or other organizations.

In addition, most states and municipal governments require that inspectors hold at least one professional certification. This involves passing detailed examinations on subjects such as construction techniques, code requirements, and building materials.

ADVANCEMENT POSSIBILITIES

Advancement possibilities in this field vary. One path is to stay with an employer and advance to senior status, earning progressively higher salaries as time passes. In larger organizations, the potential to move into a supervisory role also exists. Normally this would consist of supervising other inspectors, but it is also possible to move into more broad-based management positions, especially if additional training in business or management is completed.

Another possibility is to move from one employer to another, using one's background and experience to gain a more desirable position. For example, an inspector employed by a small city might move to a larger city where salaries are higher and experiences are more diverse.

If a career change is desired, inspectors might use business and personal contacts to pursue employment with construction companies or other employers within the building and construction industry. In such instances, completion of additional education related to the new position can be helpful.

ADDITIONAL SOURCES OF INFORMATION

American Society of Home Inspectors
932 Lee Street, Suite 101
Des Plaines, IL 60016

Association of Construction Inspectors
1224 North Nokomis NE
Alexandria, MN 56308
iami.org

Building Officials and Code Administrators International
4051 West Flossmoor Road
Country Club Hills, IL 60478
bocai.org

International Association of Electrical Inspectors
901 Waterfall Way, Suite 602
Richardson, TX 75080

International Conference of Building Officials
5360 Workman Mill Road
Whittier, CA 90601-2298
icbo.org

Southern Building Code Congress International
900 Montclair Road
Birmingham, AL 35213
sbcci.org

13

OTHER JOBS RELATED TO REAL ESTATE

The preceding chapters have outlined some of the major opportunities available to those interested in real estate careers. In addition to those focus areas, many other occupations relate in substantial ways to the real estate arena.

Following is a brief overview of some of these career areas. Some represent alternatives for those who work directly in real estate but then choose to make a career change. Others consist of entirely separate career paths that in some way involve connections with the real estate industry.

TITLE EXAMINERS AND RESEARCHERS

An important part of the real estate world is the keeping of records. Because real estate is such a valued commodity, the need to maintain various records about land, homes, commercial buildings, or other types of property has long been recognized. Governments maintain records about land for tax purposes, among other reasons, and laws designed to protect the rights of property holders require that various types of documents be created and kept on file about real estate transactions. In addition, banks and other commercial establishments also maintain documentation about real estate in which they hold some type of interest.

With all this documentation, a continuing need exists for employees who develop, maintain, or otherwise work with real estate–related records.

One such role is that of title researchers or title examiners. These specialists conduct research about property that is being considered for a possible sale or mortgage.

Tasks undertaken by title examiners all revolve around the documents involved in land ownership such as deeds, mortgages, and contracts. For example, examiners may search records to see if delinquent taxes are due or prepare title insurance policies. They review mortgages and other types of documents to verify important facts such as the legal description of property, the identity of owners, and any relevant restrictions or conformity to requirements. In the process, they write reports and correspondence, communicate with the parties involved in land transactions, and help to work out problems or conflicts.

While written records about property may be extensive, they are also prone to errors. It is a simple fact of life that in gathering or recording information, people tend to make mistakes. For example, in recording the name of a previous property holder, the first or last name might be misspelled, or the middle initial may be in error. Even a small mistake in this regard can have serious repercussions, though, because it could cause confusion with another individual or otherwise call into question a property owner's identity. Before a piece of real estate can be sold, a title researcher must verify that such mistakes do not appear in a title to the land in question. The researcher must also search for other mistakes. Some might involve wording or spelling, while others may relate to actual features of the property such as a conflict with boundaries, a problem with a water or power line, or a claim by another party regarding ownership or financial obligations.

In many cases, errors can be corrected once identified by a simple process such as filing a legal document noting the correction. In others, property owners, attorneys, or others must take more involved measures to resolve identified problems. In either case, title researchers play an important role by carefully examining the title and reporting any such problems.

REAL ESTATE CLERKS AND SECRETARIES

The need to maintain records related to real estate means that a demand exists for a number of support positions. Many agencies or other related organizations employ clerks for this purpose.

Generally speaking, real estate clerks maintain records concerned with rental, sale, or management of real estate. According to the U.S. Department of Labor, they may perform any combination of the following duties.

- Type copies of listings of real estate rentals and sales for distribution to trade publications and for use as reference data by other departments
- Compute interest owed, penalty payment, amount of principal, and taxes due on mortgage loans, using a calculating machine
- Hold in escrow collateral posted to ensure fulfillment of contracts in transferring real estate and property titles
- Check due notices on taxes and renewal dates of insurance and mortgage loans to take follow-up action
- Send out rent notices to tenants
- Write checks in payment of bills due, keep records of disbursements, and examine canceled returned checks for endorsement
- Secure estimates from contractors for building repairs
- Compile list of prospects from leads in newspapers and trade periodicals to locate prospective purchasers of real estate
- Open, sort, and distribute mail
- Submit photographs and descriptions of property to newspapers for publication
- Maintain and balance bank accounts for sales transactions and operating expenses
- Maintain a log of sales and commissions received by real estate sales agents
- Scan records and files to identify dates requiring administrative action, such as insurance premium due dates, tax due notices, and lease expiration dates
- Compose and prepare routine correspondence, rental notices, letters, and material for advertisements

Secretaries or administrative assistants tend to perform duties similar to those of clerks, but in many cases they have a broader range of duties. Their responsibilities may include not just keeping records and greeting visitors, but also other tasks including dealing with various types of office automation. They may complete complex word-processing projects, help design brochures or Web pages, keep in touch electronically with agents and brokers who are in the field, and conduct Internet-based research. In larger offices, they may also train or supervise other clerical staff.

In many real estate offices, the secretary or administrative assistant serves as the firm's information manager. Typical duties might include scheduling meetings, answering questions posed by clients or potential clients, creating correspondence and other documents, and maintaining both paper and electronic files related to the properties handled by their agency. They might also assist in marketing efforts such as creating or placing ads in newspapers, magazines, or other media, or planning open houses or other special events.

Secretarial personnel typically operate a variety of equipment such as desktop or laptop computers, fax machines, photocopiers, and telephone systems. In some offices, they play a key role in assessing technology needs and helping the firm stay current in its use of appropriate hardware and software.

Job titles in this field vary. In larger firms, titles such as executive secretary, executive assistant, administrative assistant, office manager, or senior secretary may be used. In some circles, the term "secretary" is seen as an outdated one, with "administrative professional" or similar terminology preferred.

Although a college degree may not be necessary to work as a clerk or secretary in the real estate field, specialized training is a plus. At the minimum, high school or vocational school courses in word processing and related areas are needed. Many successful clerical staff workers obtain training at a community or technical college in areas such as office systems technology or secretarial science. Most employers expect secretaries to have good skills in word processing as well as in use of software for applications such as producing spreadsheets and manipulating databases. In addition, solid skills in grammar, spelling, and oral communication are necessary.

Most secretaries, clerks, or other clerical staff tend to focus on this area of the real estate enterprise. It is not unknown, however, for those with talent and initiative to use such jobs to learn more about the business and then move into other types of real estate positions.

Increasingly, workers in this field choose to obtain special certifications to attest to their skills. For example, the International Association of

Administrative Professionals awards the designations of Certified Professional Secretary and Certified Administrative Professional to those who pass an exam and demonstrate that they meet other specified requirements.

For more information about this area, contact:

International Association of Administrative Professionals
10502 Northwest Ambassador Drive
P.O. Box 20404
Kansas City, MO 64195-0404
iaap-hq.org

ARCHITECTS

Architects are closely linked to the real estate industry. After all, it is their work that forms the basis for both renovations and new construction. They design individual buildings such as houses, churches, and office buildings; complexes such as shopping centers and factories; and other structures. Their plans form the basis for the work done by carpenters, bricklayers, and other construction specialists.

Some architects specialize in one type of structure or a single phase of work. In larger firms, such specialization may be common. For example, some architects may concentrate on planning and predesign services, while others might focus on design work.

The work of architects covers both the appearance and the functional aspects of building design. They work to see that buildings are safe, economical, and attractive, and designed to meet the specific needs of those who will occupy them.

Typically, a project undertaken by an architect entails first meeting with clients to discuss the initial ideas for a structure, and then coming up with preliminary plans based on those discussions. Then after the client reacts to the initial plans, more formal plans are developed (perhaps in several stages), and the final versions are used by construction professionals to guide their work.

In some cases, this process includes predesign services such as site selection, feasibility studies, or environmental impact assessments. In others, the emphasis is placed on developing final construction plans. Typically, such plans convey not only the proposed appearance of a structure, but also detailed drawings of electrical systems, heating and air-conditioning systems, plumbing, and the overall designs of the structure itself. Architects might also specify building materials, selection of interior furnishings, and take steps to make sure the needs of those with disabilities are addressed.

As a project develops, architects keep up with changes and work them out to the satisfaction of their clients. For example, if it becomes obvious that a portion of a building will exceed the costs originally anticipated, they may come up with an alternative design that is less costly.

In completing their work, architects make drawings, write reports, attend meetings, communicate via telephone and E-mail, and perform other related functions. To an increasing degree, their work involves the use of computers and sophisticated software for developing plans and blueprints. Much of what once required drawing by hand, in fact, is now done by computer. This necessitates mastery of computer-aided design and drafting and other advanced technologies.

In addition to developing designs and plans, architects often play the role of adviser. They may help clients in identifying possible contractors, obtaining construction bids, choosing a contractor, and negotiating a contract. They may also provide advice on areas ranging from selecting building sites to fostering energy efficiency.

Working in this field requires special training and credentialing. The typical path is to earn a college degree in the field, serve for a three-year period as an intern, and then take the Architect Registration Examination to become fully credentialed as a professional architect.

Most architects are employed in architectural firms. Some work for building contractors or government agencies. A significant number are self-employed.

For more information about architectural careers, contact:

Consortium for Design and Construction
   Careers
P.O. Box 1515
Oak Park, IL 60304-1515
archcareers.net

National Council of Architectural Registration Boards
1801 K Street NW
Washington, DC 20006-1310
ncarb.org

The American Institute of Architects
1735 New York Avenue NW
Washington, DC 20006

INSURANCE SALES AGENTS

In many ways, the insurance industry is closely related to the world of real estate. Insurance protects home owners, businesses, and other property owners against financial losses. Too, the skills used in selling insurance are not unlike those needed for success in real estate sales. For those with an interest in a possible sales career, insurance represents an area worth consideration.

Insurance sales agents help clients choose insurance policies designed to provide protection from financial loss related to property or other assets, health, or loss of life. Some work as independent agents or brokers, representing several different companies to potential and existing customers. Others, who may be known as captive agents, are employed exclusively by a single insurance company.

In addition to seeking new clients and selling additional insurance to existing customers, insurance agents perform a variety of other functions. They assist policyholders in settling insurance claims, maintain records, complete reports, and in many cases manage office operations. Many agents also sell financial products or provide advice in investing or other financial matters.

Insurance agents may deal with any of several types of insurance. They may sell life insurance, property and casualty insurance, health-care policies, or other policies and services. Some offer estate planning, retirement planning, investment opportunities, or other financial services.

Like many real estate agents, insurance sales agents often work in small offices where they meet with clients, conduct business via telephone and computer, process documents, and maintain records. They also may meet clients in their homes or places of business.

Insurance sales agents may be employed by insurance agencies or may work directly for insurance companies, banks, or other financial institutions, or they may be self-employed, operating their own agencies.

There is no uniform set of requirements for employment in this field. Many insurance agents hold college degrees in business administration, marketing, or a related field. Others have degrees in other fields (such as education or the liberal arts) and then learn the insurance business through company training programs or on-the-job experience. Some agents do not hold college degrees, but instead have a high school diploma and experience in other areas of employment. Whether or not they hold degrees, most participate in some type of formal training. This may consist of college courses in insurance or salesmanship, corporate training programs, non-credit seminars, or independent study courses, among other options.

State licensing is also required. Typically, this involves taking some specified courses and passing a written examination. Special certifications are also available through professional associations.

Personal skills include good or excellent communication abilities, solid organizational skills, computer competency, a willingness to work hard, and a strong sense of personal ethics. Ideally, insurance agents must be motivated by more than just potential earnings, but should have the best interests of their clients at heart.

For more information, contact any of the following organizations:

Independent Insurance Agents of America
127 South Peyton Street
Alexandria, VA 22314
iiaa.org

National Association of Professional Insurance Agents
400 North Washington Street
Alexandria, VA 22314

National Alliance for Insurance Education
 and Research
P.O. Box 27027
Austin, TX 78755

REAL ESTATE SPECIALTY POSITIONS

As previously noted, some real estate jobs can be found within organizations such as colleges or other nonprofit organizations that own real estate for their own operational use, or that invest in real estate as part of an endowment or other type of funding support.

For example, one statewide university system maintains the position of Real Estate Specialist. The person holding this position is responsible for providing support in real estate matters and in public records research. Duties include developing written documents related to real estate matters that are then handled by attorneys; coordinating real estate closings; reviewing closing documents and settlement statements; reviewing title commitments and surveys; drafting real estate–related correspondence; obtaining information from public records and offices; organizing appropriate documents and preparing them for filing or storage; and performing other duties as directed.

In one private university, the position of Associate Vice President for Capital Assets deals with matters such as campus development projects, capital and financial planning, purchasing land, leases, and coordinating the university's overall real estate strategy. Job duties include developing the institution's strategy for real estate, major construction projects, and capital assets throughout the university; managing real estate staff involved in the coordination of leases and building projects; overseeing building projects; establishing and maintaining relationships with outside building contractors; measuring project progress against building plans; purchasing real estate when appropriate; negotiating and preparing contracts for land to be used by the university; assisting in determining and monitoring budgets for major projects; and performing related duties.

In another university, a position of Director of Real Estate Administration is responsible for monitoring and maintaining property owned by the institution. Duties include developing and maintaining automated records and databases of office accounts, lease rentals, and repairs; maintaining tax information, maps, deeds, and other real estate documents; obtaining appraisals on real estate properties; listing and paying taxes on real property; handling insurance matters; reviewing collection of monthly rent payments on rental property; preparing reports; recommending personnel actions such as hirings, promotions, and performance appraisals; and performing other related duties.

These are just a few examples of positions in large organizations that deal primarily with responsibilities related to real estate. To determine if such positions can be found in companies or nonprofit organizations in which you may be interested, check with the human resources or personnel office.

OTHER RELATED JOBS

A variety of other jobs either relate to the real estate industry or require skills similar to those involved in some types of real estate jobs. They include the following:

- Auctioneers
- Insurance claims clerks
- Insurance claims examiners
- Landscape architects
- Law clerks
- Legal assistants
- Loan clerks
- Loan interviewers
- Paralegals
- Retail salespeople
- Sales managers
- Surveyors

If you find the real estate careers described in this book attractive, you may also wish to investigate these similar career areas.

C H A P T E R

14

EDUCATIONAL OPTIONS

As with other careers in the complex world of the twenty-first century, education is a key to success in pursuing real estate careers. Certainly it is not the only factor, and real estate holds an advantage over some professions in that initiative and experience can allow those without advanced educational backgrounds to succeed in some types of positions.

At the same time, some special training is needed. As noted earlier, agents and brokers must be licensed by the states in which they work. To become licensed, they must pass written exams, and in most cases must complete classes or seminars to prepare for these exams. Increasingly, agents and brokers hold college degrees, although this is not always required.

Options for training vary. Many real estate firms offer training programs for beginners as well as continuing education opportunities for experienced agents, with larger companies tending to offer more extensive programs than smaller ones. Local real estate associations often sponsor courses on basic real estate fundamentals and legal aspects of real estate, as well as advanced courses in areas such as mortgage financing and property management, through their affiliation with the National Association of Realtors.

Colleges and universities throughout the United States and Canada also offer programs and courses in real estate. These vary from clusters of courses or tracks within other programs (such as business administration or finance) to full-fledged real estate majors.

Many other real estate–related fields also require special training, even if licensing is not involved. Those who practice urban and regional planning, mortgage banking, or other related areas are normally expected to have completed the appropriate higher education or other type of training.

Following is an overview of educational options, including a look at representative programs. For more details on any given program, contact the college or other appropriate organization directly and request a catalog, application information, and financial aid materials, if applicable. Also, see Appendix B for a listing of colleges and universities offering real estate programs.

COLLEGES AND UNIVERSITIES

Programs offered by four-year colleges and universities include bachelor's degree programs, master's degree programs, and some doctoral-level programs for those interested in the scholarly aspects of the real estate field. Options range from degree programs emphasizing preparation for real estate careers, to components of other types of programs such as master's of business administration (M.B.A.) and bachelor's programs in finance, business, marketing, or other related areas. Other programs focus on related areas such as banking or urban and regional planning. The following listings provide a look at representative programs.

University of Alabama

Through its Culverhouse College of Commerce and Business Administration, the University of Alabama offers a major in Real Estate that covers real estate investments, land management and development of land, brokerage or sales, real estate appraisal, and real estate financing. It prepares students for positions in real estate sales, lending departments of financial institutions, urban planning, and government agencies.

Students complete a finance core with courses in financial institutions and markets, macroeconomics, and computerized management information systems; and a real estate core with courses in principles of real estate, real estate finance, real and personal property law, property management or intermediate financial management, and real estate appraisal or investments.

For more information, contact:

Culverhouse College of Commerce and Business Administration
University of Alabama
Box 870223
Tuscaloosa, AL 35487-0223
205-348-7443

Cornell University

Cornell University's program in real estate consists of two years of study during which students complete forty-two credits of required courses and twenty additional credits of elective courses. Core courses cover the following areas:

- Construction Planning
- Facility Design and Management
- Finance
- Housing Economics
- International Trade
- Marketing and Management
- Real Estate Law
- Regulation
- Urban Planning
- Statistics

For more information, contact:

Real Estate Program
Cornell University
Ithaca, NY 14853
cornell.edu

Kansas State University

Kansas State University offers a master's degree in Regional and Community Planning that can be completed with four semesters of course work and a recommended summer internship between the first and second years.

It also offers a related master of arts degree in Environmental Planning and Management.

Core courses include:

- Planning Communications
- Computer Applications in Planning 1
- Computer Applications in Planning 2
- Planning Principles
- Physical Processes of Plan Implementation
- Planning Law
- Fiscal Processes of Plan Implementation
- Planning Methods 1
- Planning Methods 2
- Planning Administration
- Community Decision Analysis
- Planning Theory, Ethics and Practice
- Community Plan Preparation

In addition to completing these courses, students complete a specialization paper in their area of expertise.

For more information, contact:

Regional and Community Planning Program
Kansas State University
Manhattan, KS 66502
785-532-5961
ksu.edu

University of California

The Haas School of Business at the University of California offers real estate courses at the bachelor's, master's, and doctoral level.

Undergraduate (bachelor's level) courses include the following:

- Real Estate Investment Analysis
- Real Estate Valuation
- Real Estate Finance

Master's (M.B.A.) and doctoral courses include:

- Real Estate Investment Analysis
- Real Estate E-Commerce
- Real Estate Development
- Real Estate Finance and Securitization
- Real Estate Management Seminar
- Urban Housing Policy
- Real Estate Doctoral Seminar
- Special Topic Seminar

Each course provides broad-based information that can help prepare students for real estate careers. For example, the Real Estate Finance course focuses on the structure and operation of the U.S. mortgage market. It covers the fundamentals of mortgage contracting, detailed aspects of residential and commercial real estate lending, and recent innovations made in ownership forms. Other course topics include methods to design mortgages to reduce risk, an overview of multitrillion-dollar mortgage derivatives and securitized asset markets, and basic principles of derivative structure and pricing. Students also gain exposure to proprietary Web technologies used in this market, experience with computerized evaluation tools, and opportunities to develop business presentation skills through class projects.

For more information about this course or other real estate courses, contact:

Haas School of Business
University of California
Berkeley, CA 94720-1900
510-643-6105
berkeley.edu

George Washington University

As a part of its Master of Business Administration degree program, the George Washington University offers a field of concentration in Real Estate and Urban Development. This program focuses on the development of analytical tools and applied problem-solving skills for use by prospective or practicing real estate professionals.

According to the university, students are enrolled in this program by organizations such as the National Association of Home Builders, National Capitol Planning Commission, National Association of Realtors, Federal Reserve Board, Mortgage Banking Association, Federal National Mortgage Association, and a variety of leading businesses.

Courses offered in this program include the following:

Real Estate Development

This fundamentals course examines the economic, social, and legal forces that shape real estate development. It emphasizes the role of the public sector as facilitator and regulator of development activity, making it a key partner in the development process. The course entails a complete overview of commercial real estate development from site acquisition through occupancy and sale.

Financing Real Estate Development

This course focuses on the financing and valuation of commercial real estate. Topics include the basics of mortgage financing and real estate lending. Land, construction, and permanent financing arrangements are analyzed using discounted cash flow analysis, and advanced principles of mortgage risk analysis and real estate securitization are examined.

Problems in Real Estate Valuation

Taught as a seminar, this course requires that all students complete a combined market and financial feasibility study on a Washington, D.C., development site. The course fits a developer investment strategy to the context of a physical property and applies analytical techniques used in market research with a risk/return cash flow analysis.

In addition to these required courses, students may choose from electives such as the following:

- Construction Project Management
- Investment Analysis
- Project Management
- Cost and Budget Analysis
- Financial Decision Making
- Market Research
- Entrepreneurship

- New Venture Initiative
- Financial Statement Analysis
- Financing State and Local Government

For more details about this program, contact:

Real Estate and Urban Development Program
Department of Finance
George Washington University
2023 G Street NW
Washington, DC 20202
202-994-7478
gwu.edu

University of British Columbia

An innovative Bachelor of Business in Real Estate degree program is offered through a collaborative effort among the Real Estate Institute of British Columbia, the University of British Columbia, and Open University.

This program is designed for working professionals in the real estate industry, allowing them to continue their careers while advancing their formal education at the same time. In this program, students take general education courses, general business courses, and a number of real estate courses such as Real Property Law, Foundations of Real Estate Mathematics, Real Estate Finance in a Canadian Context, Urban and Real Estate Economics, Real Estate Investment Analysis and Appraisal, Residential Building Construction, Commercial Building Construction, Land Use Regulation, Business Policy and Strategy with Applications to Real Estate, and Urban Studies.

For more information, contact either of the following organizations:

University of British Columbia
Real Estate Division
P.O. Box 5380
Station Terminal
Vancouver, BC V6B 5N4
604-822-8444 or 888-776-7733 (toll-free)

Open University
4355 Mathissi Place
Burnaby, BC V5G 4S8
604-431-3000 or 800-663-7911
ola.bc.ca

University of North Carolina

The University of North Carolina's Kenan-Flagler Business School offers a comprehensive and well-established program in real estate. An especially attractive feature of the master's-level program is that it offers approximately five fellowships annually.

Students take courses such as Real Property Decisions, Applied Real Property Decisions, Real Estate Development Processes, and others. Participants in these courses include students enrolled in the Department of City and Regional Planning, the executive M.B.A. program, and the university's law school. Along with the business school's real estate courses, recommended courses include finance, strategy, and marketing classes.

Typical courses taken with the real estate sequence include the following:

- Business Demographics
- Advanced Corporate Finance
- Investment Banking
- Bond and Currency Markets
- Management Consulting
- Negotiations
- Entrepreneurship and Minority Economic Development
- New Venture Creation
- Site Planning
- Economic Development

For additional information, contact:

The Kenan-Flagler Business School
University of North Carolina at Chapel Hill
Chapel Hill, NC 27599-3490
kenanflagler.unc.edu

California State University, Sacramento

Cal State Sacramento offers a bachelor's degree concentration in Real Estate and Land Use. This program prepares students for a variety of careers within the real estate industry including planning-related positions with government agencies, jobs in banks and other lending institutions, positions related to environmental regulation, and careers in real estate sales or brokerage. By completing the courses required for this concentration, students may qualify to take the California Department of Real Estate broker's exam.

Courses offered in this concentration (or available to students in this area) include:

- Real Estate Principles
- Managerial Real Estate
- Managerial Real Estate Law
- Real Estate Finance
- Market Analysis and Feasibility Studies
- The Land Use Regulatory and Entitlement Process
- Business, Ethics and Society
- Current Topics in Real Estate and Land Use
- Management of Human Resources
- Modern Portfolio Management
- The Construction Industry
- Legal Aspects of Construction
- Construction Labor Relations
- Environmental Impact Analysis: the Procedure and the Statement

The following course descriptions provide a look at just what is covered in some of these courses:

Real Estate Principles

An examination of real estate principles and practices necessary for the acquisition, financing, management, and disposition of real estate. Incidents of ownership, the brokerage business, state regulation, and transactional ethics are emphasized. Students concentrating in real estate and land use affairs are strongly advised to complete this course. Satisfactory completion of this course will entitle students to sit for the California sales-person license.

Managerial Real Estate

Presents the theory and methods of real estate asset management. Topics include site selection, real estate asset leasing, purchase, management, and disposition decisions, as well as strategy and methods in acquisition planning. Financial management for one's real estate assets and redeployment through the public sector approval, conditioning, and permitting process are emphasized.

Real Estate Finance

An examination of the mechanisms of real estate finance, sources of funds, loan contracts, principles of mortgage risk analysis, and the role of group equity investment. The evolution of secondary mortgage markets, government policy, and market interference are investigated from a risk management standpoint.

Market Analysis and Feasibility Studies

Analysis of nonfinancial and financial factors influencing investment decision making in income-producing property. Topics include location and its linkages; methods of estimating demand for real estate; methods for evaluating competing supply; use of market analysis in decision making; development of cash flow statements; alternative investment criteria; risk, legal, financing, and tax analysis; and operating, financing investment, and reversion decisions.

The Land Use Regulatory and Entitlement Process

The course focuses upon the interface of the public and private sector in California land development process, and the influence of a polycentric governmental landscape upon land use regulatory and entitlement procedures. A proactive, opportunity-oriented problem-prevention approach will be taken in addressing such topics as general plan and zoning code development and administration, environmental review process, taxation impacts, public services and infrastructure, comparative analysis of urban form and growth management, and role of the judiciary, neighborhood groups, and other participants in the land use decision-making process.

Current Topics in Real Estate and Land Use

Examines contemporary and emerging issues in land use regulation, market analysis, mortgage markets, property markets, real estate cycles, real estate development, real estate finance and investments, real estate securities, real estate portfolio management, and/or real estate taxation.

Cooperative Education Experiences in Real Estate and Land Use Affairs

In-depth supervised work experience in real estate and land use affairs. This supervised work experience allows the student to become familiar with the practices of the real estate industry and/or governmental agencies. Open to all upper-division students subject to permission of the Organizational Behavior and Environment Department.

For more details, contact:

Real Estate Program
California State University, Sacramento
6000 J Street
Sacramento, CA 95819
916-278-6011

University of Cincinnati

The University of Cincinnati offers both bachelor's and graduate programs in real estate. The undergraduate program combines a core curriculum in several basic areas of business with specialized courses in real estate. Students also are exposed to other disciplines that have an impact on the field of real estate such as construction, geography, and planning.

Bachelor's level courses include:

- Real Estate Principles
- Real Estate Finance
- Real Estate Appraisal
- Real Estate Law
- Real Estate Special Topics
- Development Methods, Cases and Negotiation

The M.B.A. with a concentration in Real Estate addresses areas such as appraisal, development, corporate real estate, leasing, brokerage, property management, and institutional investment. The program's focus is primarily commercial and industrial, with some exposure to housing policy issues.

Students who complete this program develop competencies in communication and writing skills, computer skills, negotiation skills, and problem-solving analytical skills. Their studies are based on a general business education core along with a number of real estate courses. Additionally, students will be provided with a significant amount of theory, methodology, and application case material.

Courses offered at the master's level include:

- Real Estate Finance
- Money and Capital Markets
- Real Estate Investment
- Real Estate Valuation
- Special Topics/Independent Study
- Real Estate Development Methods and Market Analysis
- Real Estate Management Strategies, Negotiation, and
  Case Analysis

An M.B.A. concentration in Construction Management is also offered.

For more details about any of these programs, contact:

College of Business Administration
University of Cincinnati
P.O. Box 210195
Cincinnati, OH 45221-0195
cba.uc.edu

COMMUNITY COLLEGE COURSES

Many community colleges offer degree or courses in real estate. For example, New Jersey's Raritan Valley Community College offers an associate (two-year) real estate degree. Offered though the college's Business Administration Department, this program is structured as an option in the Marketing degree program. It prepares students for entry-level positions in the real estate field and includes Real Estate Sales, a five-credit course that helps prepare students to take the New Jersey licensing examination.

Students take courses such as English, Accounting, Introduction to Business Administration, Real Estate Sales, Social Science electives, Business Mathematics, Real Estate Practices, Business Law I and II, Real Estate Appraisal I and II, Economics, and Real Estate Brokerage.

For more information, contact:

Raritan Valley Community College
P.O. Box 3300
Somerville, NJ 08876

FOR-PROFIT SCHOOLS

Some schools operate as for-profit enterprises. These privately run real estate schools often focus on preparation for licensing but may also provide educational opportunities for experienced professionals.

An example is Allied Real Estate School, which offers distance-education training in real estate. Information is presented through a variety of formats including software, audio- and videotapes, tutorials, and case studies. Students take interactive quizzes with immediate feedback and online final exams.

For more information, contact:

Allied Real Estate School
22952 Alcalde Drive
Laguna Hills, CA 92653
888-751-2286
alliedschools.com

Another example is the Fontaine Real Estate School in Fitchburg, Massachusetts. This school provides courses designed to prepare students to earn the Massachusetts real estate salesperson license and the Massachusetts real estate broker license. The school also addresses educational needs of practicing real estate professionals by offering courses, seminars, and publications on a wide range of real estate–related topics.

For more information, contact:

Fontaine Real Estate School
615 South Street
Fitchburg, MA 01420
978-343-4382

For information about other schools of this type, check with your state real estate licensing office. Schools can also be located through Web searches or in the yellow pages. For example, information about private schools can be obtained at the following websites:

A+ Real Estate Schools
www.aplusnow.com

Schools of Real Estate
schoolsofrealestate.com

PROFESSIONAL SOCIETIES

Professional organizations often sponsor courses, seminars, or other educational offerings. Several examples are profiled below; check with any association in which you are interested (see list in Appendix D) for details on selections, costs, schedules, and other relevant information.

National Association of Residential Property Managers

The National Association of Residential Property Managers offers a number of classes to provide professional development opportunities. These include the following:

PPM (Professional Property Manager) Operations Course

The focus of this course is mastering the basic knowledge, skills, and operational tools needed to manage residential properties effectively. It covers the property manager's responsibility in residential property development, daily management, and growth and covers topics such as rental agreements, management goals, accounting and monetary practices, liability, administrative controls, and technology.

PPM Marketing Course

An overview of the process necessary to market a property management business is provided in this course, which covers marketing techniques such as making presentations to owners and prospecting new contacts. The course also covers marketing principles specific to residential property management.

PPM Maintenance Course

The various aspects of property maintenance are covered in this course, including types of maintenance, new account maintenance, and insurance considerations. Safety considerations, maintenance tips and shortcuts, and the economics of renovations are also covered.

PPM Technology Course

Various aspects of office and information technology are covered in this course, including word processing, database systems, accounting software, and online communications. Use of hardware such as PCs, digital cameras, fax machines, and scanners is also reviewed.

PPM Tenancy Course

With a main thrust on managing tenants in residential properties, this course looks at paperwork, policies, and procedures involved in effective tenant relations. Topics include tenant screening, security deposits, record keeping, and other relevant matters.

MPM (Master Property Manager) Operating a Maintenance Company Course

Students in this course study the business skills and procedures necessary to operate a residential maintenance company. This in-depth course covers starting a company and operating, evaluating, and controlling the business, addressing topics such as accounting, record keeping, and inventory management.

MPM Risk Management Course

Focusing on risk management, this course addresses insurance needs, tort law basics, forms and contracts, and environmental areas and physical property factors affecting risk.

MPM Personnel Procedures and Employee Relations Course

Topics covered here include selection and hiring of staff, personnel procedures, employee motivation, and effective human resource administration.

For more details, contact:

National Association of Residential Property Managers
P.O. Box 140647
Austin, TX 78714-0647
800-782-3452

Society of Industrial and Office Realtors

The Society of Industrial and Office Realtors offers a number of courses providing specialized information needed for success in this area of real estate. Typical courses are held over a two or three-day period. Offerings include the following:

Course 100: Essentials of Commercial Brokerage

Offered on an intermediate level, this course focuses on fundamental issues and trends of interest to industrial and office sales and leasing professionals. Topics covered include real estate investment and finance (financial impact of a lease from both the landlord's and tenant's perspectives, reasons for users to own or lease, value of real estate and the impact a lease has on value, and reading financial statements); construction (construction techniques and terminology, electrical and mechanical system, tenant facility needs of today); and developing a marketing strategy (marketing vision; brochures, mailings, and beyond; focused, result-oriented plans).

Course 103: Mastering Lease and Contract Negotiation

Offered as an intermediate course, this course covers the following topics: lease negotiation strategies (lease clauses and their legal and negotiation implications, perspective of the lease in relation to a deal, roles of the parties to a lease, lease negotiation situations, market trends and philosophical issues, clause-by-clause analysis of standard commercial leases, and execution requirements) and negotiation skills (such as the art of negotiation, key negotiating elements, sales skills, closing techniques, and negotiation case study activity).

Course 200: Critical Components of Commercial Brokerage

Offered over a three-day period, this twenty-four-hour course is designed for those with experience in the field. It covers topics such as advanced sales skills (presentation skills, sales proposals, using multimedia, accessing the Internet, tapping networks, and developing partnerships and strategic alliances); build-to-suit development (developer's pro forma process, break-even analysis, debt coverage ratio analysis, and tenant/landlord negotiation case study activity); ethics and professional standards (code of ethical principles, standards of professional practice, case studies, and role playing); and a spokesperson training workshop (guidelines for making presentations, keys to persuasive speaking, and videotaped presentations and practice).

Course 203: Critical Components of Commercial Brokerage

Designed for students with an average of eight to ten years of experience, this course covers the following: tenant and landlord representation (advantages and disadvantages for brokers and clients; basic phases—research, negotiation, implementation, and follow-up; understanding corporations, investors, users, and institutions; landlord strategies in response to tenant representation; and advocacy); national representation (defining national representation, advantages and liabilities, philosophies of national companies and networks, obtaining assignments, making presentations, providing value-added services, compensation issues—fees and commission splits, and collection strategies and broker lien laws).

American Society of Farm Managers and Rural Appraisers

The American Society of Farm Managers and Rural Appraisers offers a number of courses and continuing education opportunities. For example, a Fundamentals of Rural Appraisal course that can be completed via the Internet offers a comprehensive introduction to rural appraising. It covers basic concepts, principles, procedures, and the valuation process. Course topics include what professional rural appraisers do, procedures followed, level of performance required in conducting the appraisal, appraisal economics, depreciation, income capitalization, sales analysis, and comparison processes.

A Principles of Farm Management course, also available through the Internet, covers topics such as the farm and ranch management profession, achieving ownership goals, real estate terminology, and rights and responsibilities of owning real estate. Other topics include contracts, leasing properties, resource inventory, conservation and management for a sustainable future, practical agricultural mathematics, economic principles, and various aspects of budgeting.

Continuing education workshops cover topics such as:

- Administrative Review of Appraisals
- Agricultural Chattel Appraisal
- Building Business Success in the New Millennium
- Federal Land Exchanges and Acquisitions
- Building Your Business
- Current Environmental Issues Affecting Real Property
- Cold Storage Valuation
- Cost Approach Valuation of Cattle Feedyards
- Discounting and Leases
- Data Analysis Seminar
- Conservation Easements
- Environment Due Diligence
- Environment, Water and Sanitation, and Agriculture
- Fractional Interests Income Approach
- Minerals Appraisal
- Permanent Planning Appraisal
- Ranch Appraisal
- Rural Business Valuation
- Real Estate Statistics
- Appraising Rural Residential Properties
- Sales Analysis
- Soil and Water Conservation

- Market Analysis in Contemporary Spreadsheets
- Special Purpose Structures
- Timber Valuation

For more details about these and other educational offerings, contact:

American Society of Farm Managers and Rural Appraisers
950 South Cherry Street, Suite 508
Denver, CO 80246-2664
303-758-3513
asfmra.org

American Banking Association

The American Institute of Banking (AIB), a division of the American Banking Association, offers an impressive array of courses for those employed in banking, including mortgage loan officers and others with close connections to the real estate industry. It enrolls over 120,000 people each year in a variety of educational programs.

Students may choose from several alternative methods of learning including traditional classroom instruction, seminars, workshops, accelerated study, correspondence study, and computer-based training. Participants may also select from a number of course combinations including professional banking diplomas in Banking, Bank Operations, Commercial Lending, Consumer Credit, General Banking, and Mortgage Lending as well as banking skills certificates in Customer Service Skills, Securities Services Skills, and Supervisory Skills. Accelerated banking courses are also available in "fast-track" covering Commercial Lending, Commercial Real Estate Finance, Consumer Lending, Global Banking, Law and Banking: Principles, Marketing for Bankers, Money and Banking, and Principles of Banking.

Through arrangements with colleges and universities, many AIB courses have been approved for college credit. As a result, students in these courses often pursue college degrees at the same time.

For more information about these and other AIB courses, contact your local AIB office (which can be identified through local banks) or contact:

American Banking Association
1120 Connecticut Avenue NW
Washington, DC 20036
800-BANKERS
aba.com

MAKING COLLEGE PLANS

If you decide to pursue a college degree in real estate or a related field, the first step is selecting the right school for you. Of course a primary consideration is whether a given college offers real estate courses or other programs in which you might be interested. Too, consider factors such as admission requirements, costs for tuition, geographical convenience, reputation for academic quality, and track records of graduates.

To obtain such information for any college in which you're interested, consult the school's catalog or other publications. A great deal of such information is also available via the Internet. Be sure to check out the college's official website as well as descriptions provided by other sources. In the process, look for evidence that the college is fully accredited, that it has positive job placement rates, and that it would be a good "fit" for you.

While considering any given college, be sure to explore different options for paying educational expenses. Don't be overwhelmed with the costs, which can range from $1,000 to $3,000 yearly at a community college to more than $30,000 a year at many private four-year colleges. If finances are a problem, you may be able to qualify for student aid. Possibilities include scholarships, grants, loans, and other types of aid. Much help is offered by state governments, private organizations, colleges and universities themselves, and the federal government. Federal sources include the following:

Pell Grants and FSEOG (Federal Supplemental Educational Opportunity Grants)

These outright awards, unlike loans, do not have to be repaid. Pell Grants, available to undergraduate students who have not earned bachelor's or professional degrees, are based on financial need, with the neediest students obtaining the largest awards. FSEOG grants, designed to help those with exceptional financial need, may be awarded to students who have also received Pell grants.

Loans

Federal Perkins loans, Stafford loans, and PLUS loans provide several types of loan options. These funds must be repaid, but the interest rate is lower than for most other types of loans. Of particular note are Stafford loans, which are available to those who may not qualify for other types of aid. They feature an interest rate that is lower than most commercial loans and a long repayment period.

Work-Study Program

The federal work-study program provides part-time jobs for college students who demonstrate financial need. Along with a source of financial assistance, it provides the opportunity to gain work experience while still in college.

HOW TO APPLY FOR FEDERAL STUDENT AID AND SCHOLARSHIPS

A detailed application must be submitted to determine if you qualify for federal student aid. You may submit the Free Application for Federal Student Aid electronically from any computer, or you can submit a paper application.

More details are available from:

Federal Student Aid Information Center
P.O. Box 84
Washington, DC 20044
800-4-FED-AID (800-433-3243)
fafsa.ed.gov

Along with government aid, be sure to check out scholarships offered by colleges, private organizations, and state-sponsored programs. In addition to general-purpose scholarships, some address special topics within the real estate world.

For example, the Community Associations Institute offers the Byron Hanke Fellowship for Graduate Research on Community Associations, which is available to graduate students addressing topics related to community associations. These $2,000 fellowships support student research projects on community associations.

To be eligible, students must be enrolled in an accredited master's, doctoral, or law program. Their major may come from any number of disciplines, and research may cover subjects such as law, economics, sociology, urban planning, or other topics as long as it pertains to community associations and common-interest communities.

For more details about this fellowship and the process of applying, contact:

CAI Research Foundation
225 Reinekers Lane, Suite 300
Alexandria, VA 22314
703-548-8600

The Institute of Real Estate Management (IREM) also offers a number of scholarship opportunities including the following:

- *The George M. Brooker Collegiate Scholarship for Minorities.* Offers tuition support for three college students (two undergraduate and one graduate) yearly who are studying real estate.
- *The Donald M. Furbush Scholarships.* Provide assistance to persons pursuing CPM or ARM designations.
- *Paul H. Rittle Sr. Memorial Scholarship.* Offers assistance for attending courses offered by the IREM.

For information, contact:

Institute of Real Estate Management
430 North Michigan Avenue
Chicago, IL 60611-4090
irem.org

C H A P T E R

15

SOURCES OF INFORMATION AND ASSISTANCE

As you learn more about the real estate profession, you will find a variety of sources of additional information. These range from government agencies to professional organizations. The latter can be particularly helpful as sources of books, journals, newsletters, and other publications. A word of advice: reading widely about any field in which you are interested is one of the most significant keys to professional success. This applies not only to students and recent graduates, but also to real estate professionals who want to continue keeping up-to-date in their fields.

Following is an overview of a number of sources where you can get additional information.

STATE REAL ESTATE AGENCIES

A great source of information about real estate, especially matters related to obtaining licenses or other legal matters, is the real estate department, commission, or similar body in your state. While the specific organization and its scope varies from one state to another, these agencies share a number of common traits, and all play important roles in the world of real estate.

A good example is the California Department of Real Estate. California's legislature passed the first real estate license law in the United States in 1917. This law, which addresses the licensing and regulation of those receiving real estate licenses, has served as a model for this type of legislation in a number of other states.

The department's operations are funded through fees charged for real estate licenses, subdivision public reports, and other permits. It is headed by a commissioner appointed by the governor. This chief executive in turn appoints a ten-member Real Estate Advisory Commission made up of six real estate brokers and four public members. The commission, presided over by the commissioner, holds public meetings at least four times a year. It consults on the department's policies and helps determine ways to meet the needs both of the public and the real estate community, and how the people of the state of California may best be served by the department, while at the same time recognizing the needs of the industry it regulates.

Not only does the commission play a key role in the actions it takes, but its communications can be helpful in many ways. For more information, check them out at dre.ca.gov.

Similar agencies in other states can also be helpful. For a list of real estate regulatory agencies in all fifty states, see the website maintained by Rental Housing On-Line at http://rhol.org/invest/real_estate_reg_agencies.htm. A similar listing for Canadian regulatory agencies is provided in Appendix C.

STUDENT ORGANIZATIONS

College students interested in real estate careers may find it advantageous to participate in student organizations focusing on professional interests. For example, students at the University of Illinois may join the Rho Epsilon chapter of the Lambda Alpha International Student Association (LAISA). Emphasizing career interests, this group offers real estate students opportunities to meet with experienced professionals, discuss job possibilities with potential employers, and network with other students and graduates.

In addition, each year Rho Epsilon publishes the *Employers' Guide to Students Seeking Employment in Real Estate and Related Fields*, a booklet listing both bachelor's and master's degree candidates. This guide is used by employers who are seeking employees for full-time professional positions, summer interns, and related opportunities.

Other similar organizations may be found at other colleges and universities or at affiliates of professional associations. For more details, check with the director of the real estate program at any college in which you are interested.

THE REAL ESTATE LIBRARY

The Real Estate Library is a comprehensive website providing access to thousands of resources related to building and maintaining real estate careers. There is no charge for accessing this information, which has been organized to meet the needs of real estate and finance professionals, buyers, and sellers. Providing approximately twenty-five main groupings of information, the library provides a wealth of information of value to real estate professionals and others interested in the field. Topics of subject headings and links to other Internet sites include continuing education, recruiting and training, buyer and seller tools, financing tools, resource library, commercial real estate, current top ten sites, real estate links, statistics and research, legal research library, real estate law, realtors by state, speakers and seminars, closing techniques, communication skills, negotiating skills, presentation skills, and more.

For more details, see the website or contact:

The Real Estate Library
1468 Santa Rosa
Eugene, OR 97404
541-689-7039
relibrary.com

URBAN PLANNING NOW!

For those interested in careers in urban or regional planning, Urban Planning Now! is a helpful website. Developed by an urban planner who focuses on neighborhood and community development, this site provides direct links to job posting pages of city, county, and consultant websites.

Organized by state, the listings allow users to search for jobs by geographic area.

To use the site, access it at urbanplanningnow.com.

COUNSELORS OF REAL ESTATE

A number of publications are offered by the Council of Real Estate (CRE). Books, monographs, newsletters, and other publications are available.

Real Estate Issues is a quarterly featuring articles on topics such as real estate ethics, investments, tenant representation, break-even analysis, environmental issues, market analysis, and capital formation. The journal is free to CRE members, and is also available to nonmembers through paid subscriptions.

The Counselor is a newsletter for CRE members offering articles on a variety of real estate topics. The most recent issue may be viewed online by anyone who visits the organization's website.

The *CRE Member Directory* provides information on the organization's more than one thousand members and can be a useful source of contact information. It may be downloaded electronically.

Monographs and books include:

- *Tenant Retail Properties: Changing Space and Capital Markets*, by Maury Seldin, CRE, and Ron M. Donohue
- *Statistical Primer for Real Estate Problem Solving*, by Norman R. Benedict, CRE, and Ted H. Szatrowski, Ph.D.
- *Real Estate Counseling in a Plain Brown Wrapper*, by Jared Shlaes, CRE
- *Real Estate and the Money Markets*, by James E. Gibbons, CRE
- *The Office Building: From Concept to Investment Reality*, by various authors with John R. White, CRE, editor-in-chief
- *Real Estate Counseling*, authored by nineteen practicing Counselors of Real Estate and covering the counseling function, the counselor-client relationship, analytical processes used in decision making, and typical problems involved in counseling clients regarding different types of property

For more information, contact:

Counselors of Real Estate
430 North Michigan Avenue
Chicago, IL 60611-4089
312-329-8427

AMERICAN PLANNING ASSOCIATION

For those interested in urban and regional planning, the American Planning Association offers a number of publications including the following:

- *Planning* (a monthly magazine)
- *Journal of the American Planning Association* (a quarterly journal)
- *Land Use Law & Zoning Digest* (a monthly law journal)
- *The Commissioner* (a quarterly newsletter)
- Planning Advisory Service (PAS) reports (six yearly)
- *In-Depth Planning Advisory Service* (PAS)
- *PAS Memo* (a monthly newsletter)

In addition, the association offers more than seven hundred books, monographs, and other titles from Planners Press.

For more information, contact:

American Planning Association
122 South Michigan Avenue, Suite 1600
Chicago, IL 60603
312-431-9100

AMERICAN SOCIETY OF FARM MANAGERS AND RURAL APPRAISERS

The American Society of Farm Managers and Rural Appraisers offers a number of helpful publications, including *FMRA News* and two especially helpful brochures, *Careers in Professional Farm Management* and *Careers in Rural Appraisal*.

For more information, contact:

American Society of Farm Managers and
    Rural Appraisers
950 South Cherry Street, Suite 508
Denver, CO 80246
303-758-3513
asfmra.org

URBAN LAND INSTITUTE

The Urban Land Institute provides a number of publications of use to urban planning professionals and others with an interest in this area.

Magazines

Urban Land is a monthly magazine covering trends and innovations in land use development, standards and conduct of land use planning and real estate development, and related topics.

Land Use Digest appears monthly on the organization's website. It provides abstracts of research and news reports taken from more than two hundred sources.

Books

The Urban Land Institute has published more than three hundred book titles including its comprehensive Development Handbook Series, which includes nine volumes totaling more than three thousand pages.

For information, contact:

Urban Land Institute
1025 Thomas Jefferson Street NW, Suite 500 West
Washington, DC 20007
202-624-7000 or 800-321-5011
uli.org

AMERICAN REAL ESTATE SOCIETY

Publications offered by the American Real Estate Society include annual research monographs as well as the following:

- *Journal of Real Estate Research*
- *Journal of Real Estate Literature*
- *Journal of Real Estate Portfolio Management*
- *Journal of Real Estate Practice and Education*

For further information, see the organization's website (aresnet.org) or contact:

Executive Director, ARES
James J. Nance College of Business
Cleveland State University
Cleveland, OH 44114

INSTITUTE OF REAL ESTATE MANAGEMENT FOUNDATION

The IREM Foundation offers an informative brochure, *Careers in Real Estate Management*, which covers matters ranging from how to get started in property and real estate management to educational information and salary figures.

To obtain a copy, contact the foundation at:

IREM Foundation
430 North Michigan Avenue
Chicago, IL 60611-4090
312-329-6008
irem.org

HOMESTORE.COM

Another source of information is Homestore.com, a website maintained by the National Association of Realtors. This site supplies online media and technology solutions to the home and real estate industry. Its offerings include listings of homes for sale, information about apartments and rentals, and technology to help home and real estate professionals work more efficiently and reach online audiences.

For more details, check out the site at homestore.com.

NATIONAL ASSOCIATION OF HOME BUILDERS

A good source of information about the housing industry is the National Association of Home Builders, which is a federation of over eight hundred state and local builders associations throughout the United States. This organization works to enhance the climate for the housing and building industry, and to promote policies that will keep housing a national priority. Members of the association include home builders and remodelers and others working in fields related to the housing industry. It regularly issues reports of interest to those involved in the real estate business.

A major role is public and government relations. In addition, the association conducts research and administers a wide variety of educational programs.

For more details, contact:

National Association of Home Builders
1201 Fifteenth Street NW
Washington, DC 20005-2800
800-368-5242 or 202-266-8200
nahb.com

COUNCIL OF REAL ESTATE BROKERAGE MANAGERS

The Council of Real Estate Brokerage Managers (CRB) offers a variety of services designed to help brokerage managers increase effectiveness, enhance their professional image, and network with other professionals. It sponsors training opportunities and provides a variety of professional development programs and information resources.

An affiliate of the National Association of Realtors, CRB is a major organization designed to serve those involved in real estate brokerage manage-

ment. Among other services, it awards the CRB (Certified Real Estate Brokerage Manager) designation to those who qualify. The designation indicates the successful completion of specified requirements and serves as an
indicator of demonstrated excellence and expertise in real estate brokerage
management.

The organization also publishes *Real Estate Business*, a bimonthly magazine providing in-depth coverage of technological advances, trends in the
industry, effective management and sales techniques, and other topics that
will help you become a top-notch manager. It also publishes a newsletter
for members; an electronic newsletter on management, leadership, and real
estate information; and an online referral directory.

For more information, contact:

Council of Real Estate Brokerage Managers
430 North Michigan Avenue
Chicago, IL 60611
800-621-8738
crb.com

A P P E N D I X

A

FURTHER READING

The complex and diverse real estate field warrants further reading for anyone who is interested in a possible career in this area. Following is a list of a number of helpful books in this field.

Burke, Barlow, John S. Meyers, and Alvina Reckman Meyers. *Fundamentals of Property Law*. Matthew Bender and Company, 1999.

Clark, Betty. *Choosing a Career in Real Estate*. Rosen Publishing Group, 2000.

Dorris, Tamara Lee, and Richard Mendenhall. *See How They Sell!: Success in Real Estate Sales*. Writers Club Press, 2001.

Edwards, Kenneth W. *Your Successful Real Estate Career*. AMACOM, 1997.

Evans, Blanche. *The Hottest E-Careers in Real Estate*. Dearborn Publishing, 2001.

Evans, Mariwyn. *Opportunities in Real Estate Careers*. VGM Career Books, 1997.

Evans, Mariwyn, and Michael B. Simmons. *Opportunities in Property Management Careers*. VGM Career Books, 2000.

Gaddy, Wade E., and Robert E. Hart. *Real Estate Fundamentals*. Real Estate Education Company, 2000.

Jaffe, Austin J., and C. F. Sirmans. *Fundamentals of Real Estate Investment*. South-Western Publishing, 1995.

Janik, Carolyn, and Ruth Rejnis. *Real Estate Careers: 25 Growing Opportunities*. John Wiley and Sons, 1994.

Masi, Mary, and Lauren B. Starkey. *Real Estate Career Starter*. Learning-Express, 2001.

Masi, Mary, and Norbert J. Stefaniak. *Real Estate Marketing: Developing a Professional Career*. Walker-Pearse Ltd., 1998.

Quinlan, Kathryn A., and Jean Wussow. *Real Estate Sales Agent*. Capstone Press, 1999.

Rabin, Edward H. H., and Roberta Rosenthal Kwall. *Fundamentals of Modern Real Property Law*. Foundation Press, 1998.

Robinson, Maxx. *So, You Want to Go into Real Estate?* Cardinal Books, 1999.

Williams, Martha R. *Fundamentals of Real Estate Appraisal*. Dearborn Financial Publishing, 2001.

A P P E N D I X

COLLEGES OFFERING REAL ESTATE PROGRAMS

The following list of U.S. and Canadian colleges is provided courtesy of the National Association of Industrial and Office Properties. For information about specific programs, check out the school's website. Note also that many of these institutions are affiliated with research institutes that offer certifications, conduct research, and provide community outreach services.

Alabama

University of Alabama, Tuscaloosa

cba.ua.edu

Programs Offered: Undergraduate major/minor in Real Estate, as well as graduate concentrations in Real Estate.

Arizona

Arizona State University, Tempe, AZ

cob.asu.edu

Programs Offered: College of Architecture and Environmental Design offers undergraduate major in Housing and Urban Development or Planning and a Master of Environmental Planning.

California

California State University, Northridge, CA

csun.edu/~busecon

Programs Offered: College of Business Administration and Economics, Department of Finance, Real Estate and Insurance offers undergraduate degree with option in Real Estate and M.B.A.

California State University, Sacramento, CA
csus.edu/obe/relua.html
Programs Offered: B.S. with concentration or minor in Real Estate and Land Use Affairs, and M.B.A. in Urban Land Development.

San Diego State University, CA
sdsu.edu/academicprog/Bsnview8.html
Programs Offered: College of Business Administration offers a B.S. in Real Estate, and an M.S. or M.B.A. with an emphasis in Real Estate.

UCLA, Los Angeles, CA
anderson.ucla.edu/acad_unit/finance/#phd_prog
Programs Offered: Graduate degree in Finance with a career track in Real Estate.

USC Geographic Information Science Certificate Program, Los Angeles, CA
usc.edu/dept/geography/learngis/descript.html
Programs Offered: Geographic Information Science (GIS) certification program.

University of California at Berkeley, Berkeley, CA
groups.haas.berkeley.edu/realestate/index.asp
Programs Offered: Haas School of Business offers B.A. and M.B.A. with concentration in Real Estate.

University of San Diego, San Diego, CA
usdbusiness.acusd.edu
Programs Offered: Undergraduates may choose area of emphasis in Real Estate. Also offers M.B.A. with area of emphasis in Real Estate.

University of Southern California, Los Angeles, CA
usc.edu/schools/sppd/lusk/academic/index.html
Programs Offered: School of Policy, Planning and Development offers
B.S. in Planning and Development, or minor in Construction
Planning and Management, or minor in Urban Planning and
Development as well as Master of Real Estate Development or Master
of Construction Management. Department of Finance and Business
Economics offers B.S. with Real Estate major or Real Property
Development and Management, Master of Real Estate Development,
M.B.A. Real Estate concentration, Master of Construction
Management, and Ph.D. in Real Estate.

Colorado

Colorado State University, Ft. Collins, CO
biz.colostate.edu/ugrad/finance.htm
Programs Offered: B.B.A. in Finance with a Real Estate concentration.

University of Colorado at Boulder, Boulder, CO
bus.colorado.edu/programs
Programs Offered: B.S. with area of application in Real Estate, M.B.A.
with Real Estate concentration.

University of Denver, Denver, CO
dcb.du.edu/burns
Programs Offered: Franklin L. Burns School of Real Estate and
Construction Management offers undergraduate and graduate degree
programs with concentrated business and management education for
the real estate and construction industries.

Connecticut

University of Connecticut, Storrs, CT
sba.uconn.edu
Programs Offered: Undergraduate, M.B.A., and Ph.D. programs in real
estate through the Center for Real Estate and Urban Economic
Studies.

District of Columbia

American University, Washington, DC
kogod.american.edu/default.asp?Parent=3&SiteMapID=3
Programs Offered: School of Business, Program in Real Estate and
Urban Development offers M.B.A.

George Washington University, Washington, DC
mba.sbpm.gwu.edu/progam/fields/re&ud.htm
Programs Offered: M.B.A. in Real Estate and Urban Development.

Florida

Florida Atlantic University, Boca Raton, FL
fau.edu/student/majors/real_est.htm
Programs Offered: B.B.A. and B.S. with Real Estate major.

Florida State University, Tallahassee, FL
cob.fsu.edu/rmi
Programs Offered: Department of Risk Management/Insurance, Real
Estate, and Business Law in the College of Business offers an
undergraduate degree in Real Estate.

University of Florida, Gainesville, FL
cba.ufl.edu/fire/programs/index.asp
Programs Offered: Undergraduate minor in Real Estate, M.B.A. with
Real Estate concentration, M.A. in Real Estate, Ph.D. in Real Estate.

University of Miami School of Law, Miami, FL
law.miami.edu/admissions/llm
Programs Offered: L.L.M. in Real Property Development.

Georgia

Georgia Southern University, Statesboro, GA
gsaix2.cc.gasou.edu/finecon/aboutus.html
Programs Offered: Department of Finance and Economics offers
undergraduate program with emphasis in Real Estate.

Georgia State University, Atlanta, GA
cba.gsu.edu/academic/index.html
Programs Offered: College of Business offers B.B.A. in Real Estate, M.S. in Real Estate, M.B.A. with major in Real Estate, and Ph.D.

Georgia Tech University, Atlanta, GA
murmur.arch.gatech.edu/bc
Programs Offered: B.S. in Building Construction with focus in Building Construction Management, Construction Development, or Construction Science. M.S. in Building Construction and Integrated Facility Management, and Ph.D. for building construction professionals.

Southern Polytechnic State University, Marietta, GA
spsu.edu/cnst
Programs Offered: Construction Department offers B.S. in Construction with General or Development concentration, M.S. in Construction, or Project Management Certificate.

State University of West Georgia, Carrollton, GA
westga.edu/~mktreal
Programs Offered: Undergraduate program in Real Estate.

University of Georgia, Athens, GA
terry.uga.edu/realestate/academic_programs
Programs Offered: B.B.A. with major in Real Estate. M.B.A. and Ph.D. in Real Estate.

Hawaii
University of Hawaii at Manoa, Honolulu, HI
cba.hawaii.edu/undergrad/realestate.asp
Programs Offered: B.B.A. in Real Estate.

Illinois
John Marshall Law School, Chicago, IL
jmls.edu
Programs Offered: L.L.M. in Real Estate Law.

Northwestern University, Evanston, IL

kellogg.nwu.edu

Programs Offered: Master of Management with Real Estate major.

University of Illinois at Urbana-Champaign, Champaign, IL

cba.uiuc.edu/finance/area.htm

Programs Offered: Offers undergraduate degree, Master of Science in Finance, and Ph.D. with concentration in Real Estate and Urban Economics.

Indiana

Indiana University, Bloomington, IN

indiana.edu/~cres/welcome.htm

Programs Offered: B.S. and M.B.A. in finance with concentration in Real Estate.

Kansas

Kansas State University

aalto.arch.ksu.edu/jwkplan/department/about/about.htm

Programs Offered: Master of Regional and Community Planning. Also offers graduate certificate program in Community Planning.

Kentucky

Morehead State University, Morehead, KY

morehead-st.edu./colleges/business/mmr/rlestop.html#topage

Programs Offered: College of Business, Department of Management, Marketing and Real Estate offers B.B.A. in Real Estate.

Louisiana

Louisiana State University, Baton Rouge, LA

bus.lsu.edu/academics/finance/programs/index.html

Programs Offered: Undergraduate and graduate degrees with Real Estate concentration.

University of Louisiana at Monroe, Monroe, LA

ele.ulm.edu

Programs Offered: College of Business Administration, Department of Economics and Finance offers concentration in Insurance and Real Estate.

Maryland

The Johns Hopkins University, Baltimore, MD
spsbe.jhu.edu/programs/grad_bus_programs.cfm?action=program
Programs Offered: School of Professional Studies and Business Education offers M.S. in Real Estate.

Massachusetts

Babson College, Babson Park, MA
babson.edu/babson/babsonhpp.nsf/public/homepage
Programs Offered: Undergraduate and master's degrees with concentration in Real Estate.

Harvard University, Cambridge, MA
gsd.harvard.edu/depts/asp
Programs Offered: Master in Design Studies with a concentration in Real Estate and Urban Development.

MIT, Cambridge, MAF
mit.edu/research/cre/msred.html
Programs Offered: M.S. in Real Estate Development.

Michigan

Ferris State University, Big Rapids, MI
ferris.edu/htmls/colleges/business/cob.htm
Programs Offered: B.S. in Insurance/Real Estate.

University of Michigan, Ann Arbor, MI
bus.umich.edu
Programs Offered: Graduate School's Urban and Regional Planning program and Business School offer dual degree of M.B.A. and Master of Urban Planning for people who want to go into urban real estate development.

Minnesota

St. Cloud State University, St. Cloud, MN
bulletin.stcloudstate.edu/ugb/programs/fire.asp
Programs Offered: B.S. in Real Estate.

University of St. Thomas, St. Paul, MN
gsb.stthomas.edu
Programs Offered: Graduate School of Business offers M.S. in Real
    Estate Appraisal and M.B.A. in Real Estate.

Mississippi

Mississippi State University, Mississippi State, MS
msstate.edu/dept/finecon/undergra.html
Programs Offered: Department of Finance and Economics offers B.B.A.
    in Real Estate and in Management of Construction and Land
    Development.

University of Mississippi, University, MS
bus.olemiss.edu
Programs Offered: B.B.A. program in Real Estate through School of
    Business Administration.

Missouri

University of Missouri, Columbia, MO
business.missouri.edu
Programs Offered: B.S.B.A. in Real Estate.

Webster University, St. Louis, MO
webster.edu/depts/business/mngt/mgthome.html
Programs Offered: Department of Business, Management Department
    offers graduate degree in Real Estate Management.

Nebraska

University of Nebraska at Omaha, Omaha, NE
cba.unomaha.edu/econ/relu.htm
Programs Offered: Department of Land Use and Economics offers
    B.S.B.A. with real estate specialization and M.A. in Land Use and Real
    Estate Economics.

Nevada

University of Nevada, Las Vegas, NV
cob.nevada.edu/cob_www/index.htm
Programs Offered: College of Business, Department of Finance offers undergraduate major or minor in Real Estate.

New Jersey

Rutgers, New Brunswick, NJ
policy.rutgers.edu/uppd
Programs Offered: Offers graduate degrees in Urban Planning and Policy Development.

Thomas Edison State College, Trenton, NJ
tesc.edu/prospective/undergraduate/degree/bsba.php
Programs Offered: B.S.B.A. in Real Estate.

New York

City University of New York, Baruch College, New York, NY
baruch.cuny.edu/ugradprograms
Programs Offered: Offers B.S. in Real Estate and Metropolitan Development.

Columbia University, New York, NY
columbia.edu/cu/academics.html
Programs Offered: Master's program in Real Estate Development in the graduate school of Architecture, Planning and Preservation. Also offers M.S. in Historic Preservation. Department of Finance and Economics offers M.B.A. with Real Estate concentration.

Cornell University, Ithaca, NY
realestate.cornell.edu
Programs Offered: Multidisciplinary Master of Professional Studies degree in Real Estate.

New York University, New York, NY
stern.nyu.edu/Academic
Programs Offered: Graduate School of Business offers M.S with concentrations in Real Estate Investment and Development, Valuation

and Analysis, International Markets, and Real Estate Finance. School for Continuing and Professional Studies offers M.S. in Real Estate, B.S. in Real Estate, Diploma in Building Construction Management, and Advanced Professional Certificate in Real Estate Studies.

North Carolina

University of North Carolina at Chapel Hill, Chapel Hill, NC
kenanflagler.unc.edu/finance/realestateconc.html
Programs Offered: Kenan-Flagler Business School Finance Department offers M.B.A. with concentration in Real Estate.

University of North Carolina, Greensboro, NC
uncg.edu/reg/Catalog/9798/bus.html#anchor20918989
Programs Offered: Undergraduate degree in Finance, Insurance and Real Estate.

Ohio

Cleveland State University, Cleveland, OH
csuohio.edu
Programs Offered: Department of Finance offers B.S., M.B.A., and D.B.A. with specialization in Real Estate. Department of Urban Studies offers Master of Urban Planning, Design and Development.

Ohio State University, Columbus, OH
fisher.osu.edu/mba/majors_minors/real_minor.html
Programs Offered: Undergraduate degree in Real Estate and Urban Analysis, and M.B.A. with a minor in Real Estate.

University of Cincinnati, Cincinnati, OH
cba.uc.edu/getreal
Programs Offered: Undergraduate and M.B.A. programs with concentration in Real Estate.

Oklahoma

University of Oklahoma, Norman OK
ou.edu/business/index2.htm
Programs Offered: B.B.A. in Real Estate.

Pennsylvania

Clarion University, Clarion, PA
clarion.edu/departments/finc
Programs Offered: B.S.B.A. in Real Estate.

Penn State University, University Park, PA
smeal.psu.edu/ire/index.html
Programs Offered: Department of Insurance and Real Estate offers
undergraduate programs in Real Estate, M.B.A. with concentration in
Real Estate, M.S. in Real Estate, and Ph.D. in Real Estate.

Temple University, Philadelphia, PA
temple.edu/bulletin/ugradbulletin/fsbm.htm#res
Programs Offered: Fox School of Business offers undergraduate degree
in Real Estate.

University of Pennsylvania. Philadelphia, PA
wharton.upenn.edu/programs.html
Programs Offered: Undergraduate, M.B.A., and Ph.D. programs in Real
Estate.

South Carolina

University of South Carolina–Columbia, Columbia, SC
darlamoore.badm.sc.edu/undergrad/undergrad.html
Programs Offered: B.S.B.A. in Real Estate.

Tennessee

University of Memphis, Memphis, TN
fcbe.memphis.edu/academichome.html
Programs Offered: B.A. in Real Estate and M.S. in Real Estate
Development.

Texas

Baylor University, Waco, TX
hsb.baylor.edu/fin/?lev3=30
Programs Offered: Undergraduate degrees in Real Estate and Regional
and Urban Studies.

Southern Methodist University, Dallas, TX
reil.cox.smu.edu
Programs Offered: Department of Insurance, Real Estate and Business
law offers undergraduate degree with major in Real Estate/Finance,
and M.B.A.

Texas A&M University, College Station, TX
business.tamu.edu/lere/mlere.html
Programs Offered: Lowry Mays College and Graduate School of
Business offers master's in Land Economics and Real Estate.
Department of Urban Planning offers master's degrees in Land
Development or Construction Management.

Texas Christian University, Ft. Worth, TX
neeley.tcu.edu/programs/undergraduate/major_fina.htm
Programs Offered: Undergraduate degree in Finance (with Real Estate
emphasis).

University of North Texas, Denton, TX
unt.edu/academicsandresearch.htm
Programs Offered: College of Business offers undergraduate, M.S., and
Ph.D. with major in Real Estate.

University of Texas at Austin, Austin, TX
bus.utexas.edu/dept/finance/programs.asp
Programs Offered: B.B.A., M.B.A., and Ph.D. with concentration in
Finance and Real Estate.

Virginia

Christopher Newport University, Newport News, VA
cnu.edu/academics
Programs Offered: B.S.B.A. in Real Estate.

Virginia Commonwealth University, Richmond, VA
bus.vcu.edu/finance
Programs Offered: Graduate Certificate in Real Estate and Urban Land
Development and M.S. in Real Estate Valuation.

Washington

Washington State University, Pullman, WA
cbeunix.cbe.wsu.edu/~wcrer/index1.html
Programs Offered: B.A. with the Real Estate option in College of
Business and Economics.

Washington State University, Spokane, WA
cbe.wsu.edu/departments/index.html
Programs Offered: B.A. in Business Administration with a Real Estate
major or minor. Professional students may pursue selected career
tracks to develop their interests in areas such as appraisal, commercial
and investment analysis, and market analysis and investments.

Wisconsin

University of Wisconsin, Madison, WI
bus.wisc.edu/default3.asp
Programs Offered: Department of Real Estate and Urban Land
Economics offers B.B.A., Master's, and Ph.D. degrees.

Canada

British Columbia Institute of Technology, Burnaby, BC
bcit.ca
Programs Offered: Diploma of Technology in Commercial Real Estate,
Associate Certificate in Building Engineering Technology.

Langara College, Vancouver, BC
langara.bc.ca/realestate/pm-011.htm
Program Offered: Property Management certificate.

McGill University, Montreal, Quebec
mcgill.ca
Program Offered: Center for Continuing Education offers AACI
(Accredited Appraiser) certificate.

Queens University, Kingston, ON
queensu.ca/surp/index.htm
Programs Offered: School of Urban and Regional Planning offers M.P.I.
degree in Land Use and Real Estate Development.

Ryerson School of Urban and Regional Planning, Toronto, ON
ryerson.ca/surp
Programs Offered: B.A.A. in Urban and Regional Planning.

St. Francis Xavier University, Antigonish, Nova Scotia
stfx.ca/tresearch
Programs Offered: Real Property Appraisal.

St. Lawrence College, Kingston, ON
sl.on.ca/fulltime/index.htm
Programs Offered: Property Appraisal and Assessment.

Saint Mary's University, Halifax, Nova Scotia
stmarys.ca/academic/commerce/finmsc
Programs Offered: Classes in real estate appraisal and investment.

Seneca College of Applied Arts and Technology, Toronto, ON
senecac.on.ca/fulltime/RPA.html
Programs Offered: Real Property Administration (Assessment and
    Appraisal).

University of British Columbia, Vancouver, BC
realestate.ubc.ca
Programs Offered: Offers a Bachelor of Business in Real Estate degree
    through their Urban Land Economics Diploma Program.

University of Guelph, Guelph, ON
uoguelph.ca/liaison/majorlist.shtml
Programs Offered: Bachelor of Commerce in Housing and Real Estate
    Management.

University of Toronto, Toronto, ON
sgs.utoronto.ca/www/sgs/sgs_dept_pla.asp
Programs Offered: School of Graduate Studies, Department of
    Geography and Planning, offers M.Sc. in Planning.

University of Western Ontario, London, ON
uwo.ca/geog/undergraduate/udegree.htm
Programs Offered: B.A. Honors Geography (Urban Development).

York University, York, ON
schulich.yorku.ca/ssb.nsf?open
Programs Offered: Schulich School of Business offers M.B.A. with
    specialization in Real Property Development.

APPENDIX

CANADIAN REAL ESTATE BOARDS AND ASSOCIATIONS

The following list of boards and associations was provided courtesy of the Canadian Real Estate Association.

Alberta

Alberta Real Estate Association
2424 Fourth Street SW, Suite 310
Calgary, AB T2S 2T4
403-228-6845 or 800-661-0231
abrea.ab.ca

Brooks Real Estate Board Co-Operative Ltd.
Box 997
Brooks, AB T1R 1B8
403-362-7000

Calgary Real Estate Board Co-Operative Ltd.
300 Manning Road NE
Calgary, AB T2E 8K4
403-263-0530
creb.com

Edmonton Real Estate Board Co-Op Listing Bureau
14220 112th Avenue
P.O. Box 25000
Edmonton, AB T5J 2R4
403-451-6666
mls.ca/boards/edmonton

Fort McMurray Real Estate Board Co-Operative Listing Bureau
9908 Franklin Avenue, Suite 200
Fort McMurray, AB T9H 2K5
780-791-1124
fortmcmurrayrealestate.com

Grande Prairie Real Estate Board
10106 102nd Street
Grande Prairie, AB T8V 2V7
780-532-4508
gpmls.com

Lethbridge Real Estate Board Co-Op Ltd.
522 Sixth Street South
Lethbridge, AB T1J 2E2
403-328-8838
mls.ca/boards/lethbridge

Lloydminster Real Estate Board Association
5009 Forty-Eighth Street, Suite 203
Lloydminster, AB T9V 0H9
780-875-6939

Medicine Hat Real Estate Board Co-Operative Ltd.
403 Fourth Street SE
Medicine Hat, AB T1A 0K5
403-526-2879
mls.ca/boards/medicinehat

Northeastern Alberta Real Estate Board Co-Op Ltd.
P.O. Box 1678, Lake Centre Plaza
Cold Lake, AB T9M 1P4
780-594-5958

Red Deer and District Real Estate Board
   Co-Op Ltd.
4922 Forty-Fifth Street
Red Deer, AB T4N 1K6
403-343-0881
rdreb.ab.ca

West Central Alberta Real Estate Board
Foothills Building, 162 Athabasca Street
Hinton, AB T7V 2A4
403-865-7511

British Columbia
British Columbia Real Estate Association
1155 West Pender Street, Suite 309
Vancouver, BC V6E 2P4
604-683-7702
bcrea.bc.ca

BC Northern Real Estate Board
2609 Queensway
Prince George, BC V2L 1N3
250-563-1236
mls.ca/boards/cariboo

Chilliwack and District Real Estate Board
9319 Nowell Street, Suite 201, Box 339
Chilliwack, BC V2P 6J4
604-792-0912
mls.ca/boards/chilliwack

Fraser Valley Real Estate Board
15463 104th Avenue
Surrey, BC V3R 1N9
604-930-7600
fvreb.bc.ca

Kamloops and District Real Estate Association
418 St. Paul Street, Suite 101
Kamloops, BC V2C 2J6
250-372-9411
mls.ca/boards/kamloops

Kootenay Real Estate Board
402 Baker Street, Suite 208, Box 590
Nelson, BC V1L 4H8
250-352-5477

Northern Lights Real Estate Board
1101 103rd Avenue
Dawson Creek, BC V1G 2G8
250-782-2412

Okanagan-Mainline Real Estate Board
1889 Spall Road
Kelowna, BC V1Y 4R2
250-860-6292
mls.ca/boards/okanaganmain

Powell River Sunshine Coast Real Estate Board
4680 Willingdon Avenue
Powell River, BC V8A 2N4
604-485-6944

Real Estate Board of Greater Vancouver
2433 Spruce Street
Vancouver, BC V6H 4C8
604-730-3000
realtylink.org

South Okanagan Real Estate Board
212 Main Street, Suite 3
Penticton, BC V2A 5B2
250-492-0626
mls.ca/boards/southokanagan

Vancouver Island Real Estate Board
6374 Metral Drive, Box 719
Nanaimo, BC V9R 5M2
250-390-4212
vireb.com

Victoria Real Estate Board
3035 Nanaimo Street
Victoria, BC V8T 4W2
250-385-7766
vreb.org

Manitoba

Manitoba Real Estate Association
1240 Portage Avenue, Second Floor
Winnipeg, MB R3G 0T6
204-772-0405
realestatemanitoba.com

Brandon Real Estate Board Inc.
907 Princess Avenue
Brandon, MB R7A 6E3
204-727-4672
breb.mb.ca

The Portage La Prairie Real Estate Board
112 Saskatchewan Avenue East
Portage La Prairie, MB R1N 0L1
204-857-4111

The Winnipeg Real Estate Board
1240 Portage Avenue
Winnipeg, MB R3G 0T6
204-786-8854
wreb.mb.ca

Thompson Real Estate Board Inc.
55 Selkirk
Thompson, MB R8N 0M5
204-778-6303

New Brunswick
New Brunswick Real Estate Association
358 King Street, Suite 301
Fredericton, NB E3B 1E3
506-459-8055

Saint John Real Estate Board Inc.
600 Main Street, Suite 120
Building C, Hilyard Place
Saint John, NB E2K 1J5
506-634-8772
sjreb.com

Greater Moncton Real Estate Board Inc.
107 Cameron Street
Moncton, NB E1C 5Y7
506-857-8200
mls.ca/boards/moncton

Northern New Brunswick Real Estate Board Inc.
P.O. Box 185, Suite 5
360 Parkside Drive
Bathurst, NB E2A 3Z2
506-548-3045

The Real Estate Board of Fredericton Area Inc.
544 Brunswick Street
Fredericton, NB E3B 1Y5
506-458-8163
brunnet.net/freb

Valley Real Estate Board Inc.
56 Church Street
Edmunston, NB E3V 1J5
506-735-552
valleyboard.com

Newfoundland

Newfoundland Real Estate Association
251 Empire Avenue
St. John's, NF A1C 3H9
709-726-5110

Central Newfoundland Real Estate Board
306 Airport Boulevard
Gander, NF A1V 2L4
709-256-3248

Humber Valley Real Estate Board
P.O. Box 532
Corner Brook, NF A2H 6E6
709-634-9400

St. John's Real Estate Board
251 Empire Avenue, Second Floor
St. John's, NF A1C 3H9
709-726-5110

Nova Scotia

Nova Scotia Association of Realtors
7 Scarfe Court
Dartmouth, NS B3B 1W4
902-468-2515
nsar.ns.ca

Annapolis Valley Real Estate Board
P.O. Box 117, 2110 Highway 1
Auburn, NS B0P 1A0
902-847-9336

Yarmouth Real Estate Board
255 Main Street, Suite 200
Yarmouth, NS B5A 1E2
902-742-4545

Northwest Territories

Yellowknife Real Estate Board
5204 Fiftieth Avenue, Suite 201
Yellowknife, NT X1A 1E2
867-920-4624

Ontario

Ontario Real Estate Association
99 Duncan Mill Road
Don Mills (Toronto), ON M3B 1Z2
416-445-9910
orea.com

Bancroft District Real Estate Board
P.O. Box 1522
141 Hastings Street North
Bancroft, ON K0L 1C0
613-332-3842
bancroftrealestate.on.ca

Barrie and District Real Estate Board Inc.
85 Ellis Drive
Barrie, ON L4M 8Z3
705-739-4650
barrie-mls.on.ca

Brantford Regional Real Estate Association
106 George Street
Brantford, ON N3T 2Y4
519-753-0308

Chatham-Kent Real Estate Board
188 Saint Clair Street, P.O. Box 384
Chatham, ON N7M 5K5
519-352-4351
mls.ca/boards/chatham/home.htm

Cobourg-Port Hope District Real Estate Board
1011 William Street, Suite 23, Victoria Place
Cobourg, ON K9A 5J4
905-372-8630
eagle.ca/realestate

Cornwall and District Real Estate Board
25 Cumberland Street
Cornwall, ON K6J 4G8
613-932-6457
mls.ca/boards/cornwall

Durham Region Real Estate Board
50 Richmond Street East, Unit 14
Oshawa, ON L1G 7C7
905-723-8184

Georgian Triangle Real Estate Board
54 Third Street
Collingwood, ON L9Y 1K3
705-445-7295
mls.ca/boards/georgiantriangle

Grey Bruce-Owen Sound Real Estate Board
504 Tenth Street
Hanover, ON N4N 1R1
519-364-3827
homesacrosscanada.com

Guelph and District Real Estate Board
400 Woolwich Street
Guelph, ON N1H 3X1
519-824-7270

Hamilton-Burlington and District Real Estate Board
505 York Boulevard
Hamilton, ON L8R 3K4
905-529-810
hbdreb@on.ca

Huron and Perth County Real Estate Board
91 Brunswick Street
Stratford, ON N5A 3L9
519-271-6870
quadro.net/~perthreb

Kingston and Area Real Estate Association
720 Arlington Park Place
Kingston, ON K7M 8H9
613-384-0880

Kitchener-Waterloo Real Estate Board Inc.
540 Riverbend Drive
Kitchener, ON N2K 3S2
519-576-1400
mls.ca/boards/kwreb

Kawartha Lakes Real Estate Association Inc.
31 Kent Street East
Lindsay, ON K9V 2C3
705-324-4515

London and St. Thomas Real Estate Board
342 Commissioners Road West
London, ON N6J 1Y3
519-641-1400
http://realtors.mls.ca/london

Midland-Penetang District Real Estate Board
P.O. Box 805
Midland, ON L4R 4P4
705-526-8706

Mississauga Real Estate Board
3355 The Collegeway, Unit 29
Mississauga, ON L5L 5T3
905-608-6732
mbrea.ca

Muskoka and Halliburton Association of Realtors
18 Chaffey Street
Huntsville, ON P1H 1K7
705-788-1504

Niagara Falls–Fort Erie Real Estate Association
P.O. Box 456, 4411 Portage Road
Niagara Falls, ON L2E 6V2
905-356-7593

North Bay Real Estate Board
926 Cassells Street
North Bay, ON P1B 4A8
705-472-6812

Orangeville and District Real Estate Board
228 Broadway Avenue
Orangeville, ON L9W 1K5
519-941-4547

Orillia and District Real Estate Board Inc.
100 Coldwater Street East, P.O. Box 551
Orillia, ON L3V 6K2
705-325-9958
mls.ca/boards/orillia

Ottawa Real Estate Board
1826 Woodward Drive
Ottawa, ON K2C 0P7
613-225-2240
ottawarealestate.org

Parry Sound Real Estate Board
43 James Street
Parry Sound, ON P2A 1T6
705-746-4020

Peterborough and the Kawarthas Association of Realtors Inc.
Box 1330, 273 Charlotte Street
Peterborough, ON K9J 7H5
705-745-5724
mls.ca/boards/peterborough

Quinte and District Real Estate Board
General Delivery, P.O. Box 128
Cannifton, ON K0K 1K0
613-969-7873
quinterealestate.on.ca

Real Estate Board of Cambridge Inc.
75 Ainslie Street North
Cambridge, ON N1R 3J7
519-623-3660

Renfrew County Real Estate Board
377 Isabella Street
Pembroke, ON K8A 5T4
613-735-5840
ottawarealestate.org

Rideau–St. Lawrence Real Estate Board
1275 Kensington Parkway, Unit 12
Brockville, ON K6V 6C3
613-342-3103

Sarnia-Lambton Real Estate Board
555 Exmouth Street
Sarnia, ON N7T 5P6
519-336-6871

Sault Sainte Marie Real Estate Board
498 Queen Street East, Suite 1
Sault Sainte Marie, ON P6A 1Z8
705-949-4560

Simcoe and District Real Estate Board
44 Young Street
Simcoe, ON N3Y 1Y5
519-426-4454

St. Catharines–Welland District Real Estate Board
116 Niagara Street
St. Catharines, ON L2R 4L4
905-684-9459
mls-niagara.com

Sudbury Real Estate Board
190 Elm Street West
Sudbury, ON P3C 1V3
705-673-3388

The Brampton Real Estate Board
35 Vankirk Drive, Unit 10
Brampton, ON L7A 1A6
905-791-9913
breb.org

The Oakville Milton and District Real Estate Board
125 Navy Street
Oakville, ON LJ6 2Z5
905-844-6491
omdreb.on.ca

Thunder Bay Real Estate Board
1135 Barton Street
Thunder Bay, ON P7B 5N3
807-623-8422

Tillsonburg District Real Estate Board
Box 35, 1 Library Lane
Tillsonburg, ON N4G 4H3
519-842-9361

Timmins Real Estate Board
7 Balsam Street South
Timmins, ON P4N 2C7
705-268-5451

Toronto Real Estate Board
1400 Don Mills Road
Don Mills, ON M3B 3N1
416-443-8100
realestate.ca/toronto/home.htm

Windsor–Essex County Real Estate Board
3005 Marentette Avenue
Windsor, ON N8X 4G1
519-966-6432
windsorrealestate.com

Woodstock-Ingersoll and District Real Estate Board
65 Springbank, Unit 6
Woodstock, ON N4S 8V8
519-539-3616

York Region Real Estate Board
27 Main Street North
Newmarket, ON L3Y 3Z6
905-895-7624
realestate.ca/toronto/home.htm

Prince Edward Island

Prince Edward Island Real Estate Association
75 St. Peter's Road
Charlottetown, PE C1A 5N7
902-368-8451

Quebec

Federation des Chambres immobilières du Quebec
600 chemin du Golf
Ile-des-Soeurs, QC H3E 1A8
514-762-0212
fciq@cigm.qc.ca

Chambre immobilière de Quebec
990 av Holland
Quebec, QC G1S 3T1
418-688-3362
ciq.qc.ca

Chambre immobilière de l'Abitibi-Temiscamingue Inc.
80 Monseigneur Tessier est, Bureau 201
Rouyn-Noranda, QC J9X 3B9
819-762-1777
ciat.qc.ca

Chambre immobilière de l'Estrie Inc.
22 rue Robidoux
Sherbrooke, QC J1J 2W1
819-566-7616

Chambre immobilière de l'Outaouais Inc.
197 boul St-Josepsh
Hull, QC J8Y 3X2
819-771-5221
immeuble.outaouais.qc.ca

Chambre immobilière de la Haute Yamaska Inc.
96, rue Principale, bureau 104
Granby, QC J2G 2T4
450-378-6702

Chambre immobilière de la Mauricie Inc.
1640, 6e rue, Suite 102
Trois-Rivières, QC G8Y 5B8
819-379-9081

Chambre immobilière de Lanaudière Inc.
765, boul Manseau
Joliette, QC J6E 2E8
450-759-8511

Chambre immobilière de St-Hyacinthe Inc.
CP 667
St-Hyacinthe, QC J2S 7P5
450-799-2210

Chambre immobilière des Laurentides
555 boul Ste-Adele, Bureau 204
Ste-Adele, QC J8B 1A7
450-229-3511
mls.ca/boards/laurentides

Chambre immobilière du Centre du Quebec Inc.
355 boul St-Joseph, Local 46
Drummondville, QC J2C 2B1
819-477-1033

Chambre immobilière du Grand Montreal
600 ch du Golf
Ile-des-Soeurs, QC H3E 1A8
514-762-2440
mls.ca/boards/montreal

Chambre immobilière du Saguenay-Lac-St-Jean Inc.
2655 boul du Royaume, Bureau 490
Jonquière, QC G7S 4S9
418-548-8808
immobiliersaguenay.com

Chambre immobilière Est du Quebec Inc.
216 rue de la Cathedrale, Bureau 6
Rimouski, QC, G5L 5J2
418-723-5393

Saskatchewan

Saskatchewan Real Estate Association
231 Robin Crescent
Saskatoon, SK S7L 6M8
306-373-3350

Association of Battlefords Realtors
1101 101st Street, Suite 501, P.O. Box 611
North Battleford, SK S9A 2Y7
306-445-6300

Association of Regina Realtors Inc.
1854 McIntyre Street
Regina, SK S4P 2P9
306-791-2700
reginarealtors.com

Estevan Real Estate Board
Box 445
Estevan, SK S4A 2A4
306-634-7885

Melfort Real Estate Board
P.O. Box 21
Melfort, SK S0E 1A0
306-752-9316

Moose Jaw Real Estate Board
79 Hochelaga Street West
Moose Jaw, SK S6H 2E9
306-693-9544

Prince Albert Real Estate Board
218B South Industrial Drive
Prince Albert, SK S6V 7L8
306-764-8755
mls.ca/boards/princealbert

Swift Current Real Estate Association Inc.
12 Cheadle Street West, Suite 211
Swift Current, SK S9H 0A9
306-773-4326

Saskatoon Real Estate Board
1149 Eighth Street East
Saskatoon, SK S7H 0S3
306-244-4453
sreb.com

Weyburn Real Estate Board
33 Fifth Street, Suite 1
Weyburn, SK S4H 0Y9
306-842-0300

Yorkton Real Estate Association Inc.
41 Broadway West, Suite 40
Yorkton, SK S3N 0L6
306-783-3067

Yukon
Yukon Real Estate Association
P.O. Box 5292
Whitehorse, YK Y1A 4Z2
867-668-2070
yrea.yk.ca

APPENDIX D

SELECTED PROFESSIONAL ASSOCIATIONS

American Association of Small Property Owners
Georgetown Place
1101 Thirtieth Street NW, Suite 500
Washington, DC 20007
202-625-8330
smallpropertyowner.com

American Banking Association
1120 Connecticut Avenue NW
Washington, DC 20036
800-BANKERS
aba.com

American Institute of Architects
173 New York Avenue NW
Washington, DC 20006
aisnline.com

American Planning Association (Chicago office)
122 South Michigan Avenue, Suite 1600
Chicago, IL 60603
planning.org

American Planning Association (Washington office)
1776 Massachusetts Avenue NW
Washington, DC 20036

American Society of Appraisers
P.O. Box 17265
Washington, DC 20041
800-ASU-VALU
appraisers.org

American Society of Farm Managers and Rural Appraisers
950 South Cherry Street, Suite 508
Denver, CO 80246-2664
303-758-3513
asfmra.org

Association of Real Estate License Law Officials
P.O. Box 230159
Montgomery, AL 36123-0159
arello.com

Building Owners and Managers Association International
1201 New York Avenue NW, Suite 300
Washington, DC 20005
202-408-2662
boma.org

Community Associations Institute
225 Reinekers Lane, Suite 300
Alexandria, VA 22314
703-548-8600

Counselors of Real Estate
430 North Michigan Avenue
Chicago, IL 60611-4089
312-329-8427

Council of Real Estate Brokerage Managers
430 North Michigan Avenue
Chicago, IL 60611
800-621-8738
crb.com

Federal Housing Finance Board
1777 F Street NW
Washington, DC 20006-5210
202-408-2500

Independent Insurance Agents of America
127 South Peyton Street
Alexandria, VA 22314
iiaa.org

IREM Foundation
430 North Michigan Avenue
Chicago, IL 60611-4090
irem.org

National Association of Home Builders
1201 Fifteenth Street NW
Washington, DC 20005-2800
800-368-5242, ext. 0, or 202-266-8200
nahb.com

National Association of Housing and Redevelopment Officials
630 Eye Street NW
Washington DC 20001
877-866-2476 (toll-free) or 202-289-3500

National Association of Professional Insurance Agents
400 North Washington Street
Alexandria, VA 22314

National Alliance for Insurance Education and Research
P.O. Box 27027
Austin, TX 78755

National Association of Realtors
700 Eleventh Street NW
Washington, DC 20001
realtor.org

National Association of Residential Property Managers
P.O. Box 140647
Austin, TX 78714-0647
800-782-3452

The Urban Land Institute
1025 Thomas Jefferson Street NW, Suite 500 West
Washington, DC 20007
202-624-7000 or 800-321-5011
uli.org

Women's Council of Realtors
430 North Michigan Avenue
Chicago IL 60611
800-245-8512

GLOSSARY

Many of the terms in this glossary are provided courtesy of the Canadian Real Estate Association and the U.S. Department of Housing and Urban Development.

Adjustable rate mortgage (ARM). A type of mortgage rate loan whose interest rate changes periodically up or down, usually once or twice a year.

Amortization. Paying off a debt, such as a mortgage, by installments. The conventional amortization period for a mortgage is anywhere between fifteen and thirty years. The shorter the amortization period, the less interest you have to pay.

Annual percentage rate (APR). Everything financed in a mortgage loan package (interest, loan fees, points, or other charges) expressed as a percentage of the loan amount (usually slightly above the actual interest rate alone).

Appraisal. An estimate of a property's value.

Asking (list) price. The price placed on the property for sale by the seller.

Assumable loan. A loan that the lender is willing to transfer from the previous owner of the home to the new owner, sometimes at the same interest rate, sometimes at a new rate.

Assessor. A government official who is responsible for determining the value of a property for the purpose of taxation.

Assumable mortgage. A mortgage that can be transferred from a seller to a buyer; once the loan is assumed by the buyer, the seller is no longer responsible for repaying it.

Balloon mortgage. A mortgage that typically offers low rates for an initial period of time (usually five, seven, or ten years); after that time period elapses, the balance is due or is refinanced by the borrower.

Bankruptcy. A federal law whereby a person's assets are turned over to a trustee and used to pay off outstanding debts; this usually occurs when someone owes more than he or she has the ability to repay.

Blended payments. Payments consisting of principal and interest components, paid during the amortization period of a mortgage.

Borrower. A person who has been approved to receive a loan and is then obligated to repay it and any additional fees according to the loan terms.

Broker. A person licensed by the state, provincial, or territorial government to trade in real estate. Real estate brokers may form companies or offices that appoint sales representatives to provide services to the seller or buyer, or they may provide the same services themselves. In some cases, brokers are referred to as agents.

Building code. Based on agreed-upon safety standards within a specific area, a building code is a regulation that determines the design, construction, and materials to be used in building.

Buyer's agent (also known as *buyer's broker* or *purchaser's agent*). A person or firm representing the buyer. A buyer's agent's primary allegiance is to the buyer who is his or her client.

Certificate of title. A document provided by a qualified source (such as a title company) that shows the property legally belongs to the current owner; before the title is transferred at closing, it should be clear and free of all liens or other claims.

Client. The person being represented by an agent. The agent owes the client the duties of utmost care, integrity, confidentiality, and loyalty.

Closing. The time at which the property is formally sold and transferred from the seller to the buyer; at this time the borrower takes on the loan obligation, pays all closing costs, and receives title from the seller (also known as *settlement*).

Closing costs. Costs that the buyer must pay at the time of closing in addition to the down payment, including points, mortgage insurance premium, home-owners insurance, prepayments for property taxes, and other costs. Closing costs tend to average 3 to 4 percent of the loan amount.

CMHC. Canada Mortgage and Housing Corporation. A Canadian government corporation providing information services and mortgage loan insurance.

Commission. An amount agreed to by the seller and the real estate broker/agent and stated in the listing agreement. It is payable to the broker/agent on closing and shared, if applicable, among those salespeople involved in the sale.

Condominium. A form of ownership in which individuals purchase and own a unit of housing in a multiunit complex; the owner also shares financial responsibility for common areas.

Conventional loan. A loan that is not guaranteed or insured by the U.S. government.

Cooperative (co-op). An arrangement in which residents purchase stock in a cooperative corporation that owns a structure; each stockholder is then entitled to live in a specific unit of the structure and is responsible for paying a portion of the loan.

Contingency. A condition put on an offer to buy a home, such as the prospective buyer making an offer contingent on his or her sale of a present home.

Conventional mortgage. A private sector loan; this type of mortgage is not insured by either the Federal Housing Administration (FHA) or the Department of Veterans Affairs (VA), and thus usually requires a 10 to 20 percent down payment.

CREA. The Canadian Real Estate Association. A national association representing the real estate industry on federal public policy matters and providing member services and education. CREA promotes adherence to a strict code of ethics and standards of business practice.

Credit bureau score. A numerical rating representing the possibility a borrower may default; it is based upon credit history and is used to determine ability to qualify for a mortgage loan.

Credit history. The history of an individual's debt payment, used by lenders to gauge a potential borrower's ability to repay a loan.

Credit report. A record that lists all past and present debts and the timeliness of their repayment; it documents an individual's credit history.

Debt-service ratio. The measurement of debt payments to gross household income that may include, in addition to the main wage earner's salary, salaries of other wage earners, commissions, bonuses, overtime, etc. May also be known as *debt-to-income ratio*.

Deed-in-lieu. To avoid foreclosure ("in lieu" of foreclosure), a deed is given to the lender to fulfill the obligation to repay the debt; this process doesn't allow the borrower to remain in the house but helps avoid the costs, time, and effort associated with foreclosure.

Default. Failure to pay monthly mortgage payments in a timely manner or to otherwise meet the mortgage terms.

Delinquency. The failure of a borrower to make timely mortgage payments under a loan agreement.

Discount point. Normally paid at closing and generally calculated to be equivalent to 1 percent of the total loan amount, discount points are paid to reduce the interest rate on a loan.

Down payment. The portion of a home's purchase price that is paid in cash and is not part of the mortgage loan.

Dual agent. A real estate broker or salesperson who acts as agent for both the seller and the buyer in the same transaction. Both buyer and seller are the agent's clients.

EEM. Energy Efficient Mortgage; an FHA program that helps home buyers save money on utility bills by enabling them to finance the cost of adding energy-efficiency features to a new or existing home as part of the home purchase.

Equity. An owner's financial interest in a property; calculated by subtracting the amount still owed on the mortgage loan(s) from the fair market value of the property.

Earnest money. Funds put down by a potential buyer to show that he or she is serious about purchasing the home; it becomes part of the down payment if the offer is accepted, is returned if the offer is rejected, or is forfeited if the buyer pulls out of the deal.

Escrow account. A separate account into which the lender puts a portion of each monthly mortgage payment; an escrow account provides the funds needed for such expenses as property taxes, home-owner's insurance, or mortgage insurance.

Fair Housing Act. A law that prohibits discrimination in all facets of the home-buying process on the basis of race, color, national origin, religion, sex, familial status, or disability.

Fair market value. The hypothetical price that a willing buyer and seller will agree upon when they are acting freely, carefully, and with complete knowledge of the situation.

Fannie Mae. Federal National Mortgage Association (FNMA); a federally chartered enterprise owned by private stockholders that purchases residential mortgages and converts them into securities for sale to investors; by purchasing mortgages, Fannie Mae supplies funds that lenders may loan to potential home buyers.

FHA. Federal Housing Administration; established in 1934 to advance home ownership opportunities for all Americans; assists home buyers by providing mortgage insurance to lenders to cover most losses that may occur when a borrower defaults; this encourages lenders to make loans to borrowers who might not qualify for conventional mortgages.

FHA financing. Financing for a loan that will be insured against loss by the Federal Housing Administration. This financing requires a smaller down payment than most conventional loans.

Financial institutions. Banks, credit unions, insurance brokers, or trust companies.

Fixed-rate mortgage. A mortgage with payments that remain the same throughout the life of the loan because the interest rate and other terms are fixed and do not change.

Flood insurance. Insurance that protects home owners against losses from a flood; if a home is located in a flood plain, the lender will require flood insurance before approving a loan.

Foreclosure. A legal process in which mortgaged property is sold to pay the loan of the defaulting borrower.

Freddie Mac. Federal Home Loan Mortgage Corporation (FHLMC); a federally chartered corporation that purchases residential mortgages, securitizes them, and sells them to investors; this provides lenders with funds for new home buyers.

Ginnie Mae. Government National Mortgage Association (GNMA); this government-owned corporation is overseen by the U.S. Department of Housing and Urban Development. Ginnie Mae pools FHA-insured and VA-guaranteed loans to back securities for private investment; as with Fannie Mae and Freddie Mac, the investment income provides funding that may then be lent to eligible borrowers by lenders.

GE Capital Mortgage Insurance Company. This company is the one private-sector source of mortgage insurance to lenders in Canada.

Good faith estimate. An estimate of all closing fees including prepaid and escrow items as well as lender charges; must be given to the borrower within three days after submission of a loan application.

Gross debt service. The amount of money needed to pay principal, interest, taxes, and sometimes, energy costs.

Gross debt-service ratio. Gross debt service divided by household income.

Home inspection. An examination of the structure and mechanical systems to determine a home's safety; makes the potential home buyer aware of any repairs that may be needed.

Home warranty. Offers protection for mechanical systems and attached appliances against unexpected repairs not covered by home-owners insurance; coverage extends over a specific time period and does not cover the home's structure.

Home-owner's insurance. An insurance policy that combines protection against damage to a dwelling and its contents with protection against claims of negligence or inappropriate action that result in someone's injury or property damage.

Housing counseling agency. Provides counseling and assistance to individuals on a variety of issues, including loan default, fair housing, and home buying.

HUD. The U.S. Department of Housing and Urban Development; established in 1965, HUD works to create a decent home and suitable living environment for all Americans; it does this by addressing housing needs, improving and developing American communities, and enforcing fair housing laws.

Index. A measurement used by lenders to determine changes to the interest rate charged on an adjustable rate mortgage.

Interest rate. The amount of interest charged on a monthly loan payment; usually expressed as a percentage.

Lease purchase. Assists low- to moderate-income home buyers in purchasing a home by allowing them to lease a home with an option to buy; the rent payment is made up of the monthly rental payment plus an additional amount that is credited to an account for use as a down payment.

Lien. A legal claim against property that must be satisfied when the property is sold.

Loan. Money borrowed that is usually repaid with interest.

Listing agreement. The legal agreement between the listing broker and the seller setting out the services to be rendered, describing the property for sale, and stating the terms of payment. A commission is generally payable to the broker upon closing.

Loan fraud. Purposely giving incorrect information on a loan application in order to better qualify for a loan; may result in civil liability or criminal penalties.

Loan origination fee. A fee charged by the lender for evaluating, preparing, and submitting a proposed mortgage loan.

Loan-to-value (LTV) ratio. A percentage calculated by dividing the amount borrowed by the price or appraised value of the home to be purchased; the higher the LTV, the less cash a borrower is required to pay as down payment.

Lock-in. Since interest rates can change frequently, many lenders offer an interest rate lock-in that guarantees a specific interest rate if the loan is closed within a specific time.

Loss mitigation. A process to avoid foreclosure; the lender tries to help a borrower who has been unable to make loan payments and is in danger of defaulting on his or her loan.

Margin. An amount the lender adds to an index to determine the interest rate on an adjustable rate mortgage.

Mortgage. A lien on the property that secures the promise to repay a loan.

Mortgage banker. A company that originates loans and resells them to secondary mortgage lenders like Fannie Mae or Freddie Mac.

Mortgage broker. A firm that originates and processes loans for a number of lenders.

Mortgage insurance. A policy that protects lenders against some or most of the losses that can occur when a borrower defaults on a mortgage loan; mortgage insurance is required primarily for borrowers with a down payment of less than 20 percent of the home's purchase price.

Mortgage modification. A loss mitigation option that allows a borrower to refinance and/or extend the term of the mortgage loan and thus reduce the monthly payments.

Mortgage insurance premium (MIP). A charge paid by the borrower (usually as part of the closing costs) to obtain financing, especially when making a down payment of less than 20 percent of the purchase price, for example on an FHA-insured loan in the United States. In Canada, high-ratio mortgages (those representing greater than 75 percent of the property value) must be insured against default by either CMHC or private insurers.

Mortgagee. The person or financial institution lending the money secured by a mortgage.

Mortgagor. The property owner borrowing the money secured by a mortgage.

Offer. An indication by a potential buyer of a willingness to purchase a home at a specific price; generally put forth in writing.

Origination. The process of preparing, submitting, and evaluating a loan application; generally includes a credit check, verification of employment, and a property appraisal.

Origination fee. The charge for originating a loan; is usually calculated in the form of points and paid at closing.

Partial claim. A loss mitigation option offered by the FHA that allows a borrower, with help from a lender, to get an interest-free loan from HUD to bring mortgage payments up to date.

PITI. Principal, interest, taxes, and insurance—the four elements of a monthly mortgage payment; payments of principal and interest go directly toward repaying the loan while the portion that covers taxes and insurance (home-owner's and mortgage insurance, if applicable) goes into an escrow account to cover the fees when they are due.

PMI. Private mortgage insurance; privately owned companies that offer standard and special affordable mortgage insurance programs for qualified borrowers.

Preapprove. Lender commits to lend to a potential borrower; commitment remains as long as the borrower still meets the qualification requirements at the time of purchase.

Pre-foreclosure sale. Allows a defaulting borrower to sell the mortgaged property to satisfy the loan and avoid foreclosure.

Prequalify. A lender informally determines the maximum amount an individual is eligible to borrow.

Premium. An amount paid on a regular schedule by a policyholder that maintains insurance coverage.

Prepayment. Payment of the mortgage loan before the scheduled due date; may be subject to a prepayment penalty.

Point. An amount equal to 1 percent of the principal amount being borrowed. The lender may charge the borrower several "points" in order to provide the loan.

Property taxes. Taxes (based on the assessed value of the home) paid by the home owner for community services such as schools, public works, and other costs of local government. Normally paid as a part of the monthly mortgage payment.

Real estate agent. An individual who is licensed to negotiate and arrange real estate sales; works for a real estate broker.

REALTOR. A real estate agent or broker who is a member of the National Association of Realtors and its local and state associations.

Real property. Real estate, which may include office buildings, houses, condominiums, apartments, undeveloped land, retail stores, industrial properties, and golf courses.

Refinancing. Paying off one loan by obtaining another; refinancing is generally done to secure better loan terms (like a lower interest rate) or to roll other expenses such as costs of rehabilitation and home purchase into one.

Rehabilitation mortgage. A mortgage that covers the costs of rehabilitating (repairing or improving) a property; some rehabilitation mortgages—like FHA's 203(k)—allow a borrower to roll the mortgage loan into the new loan as well.

RESPA. Real Estate Settlement Procedures Act; a law protecting consumers from abuses during the residential real estate purchase and loan process by requiring lenders to disclose all settlement costs, practices, and relationships.

Seller's agent. The seller's agent represents the seller and does not represent the buyer.

Settlement. Another name for *closing*.

Special forbearance. A loss mitigation option where the lender arranges a revised repayment plan for the borrower that may include a temporary reduction or suspension of monthly loan payments.

Survey. A property diagram that indicates legal boundaries, easements, encroachments, rights of way, improvement locations, and so forth.

Sweat equity. Using labor to build or improve a property as part of the down payment.

Title insurance. Insurance that protects the lender against any claims that arise from arguments about ownership of the property; also available for home buyers.

Title search. A check of public records to be sure that the seller is the recognized owner of the real estate and that there are no unsettled liens or other claims against the property.

Truth-in-Lending. A federal law obligating a lender to give full written disclosure of all fees, terms, and conditions associated with the loan.

Two-step mortgage. A type of adjustable rate mortgage that has one interest rate for a predetermined initial period and then adjusts to another rate that lasts for the term of the loan.

Underwriting. The process of analyzing a loan application to determine the amount of risk involved in making the loan; it includes a review of the potential borrower's credit history and a judgment of the property's value.

Variable-rate mortgage. A mortgage in which payments are fixed, but the interest rate moves in response to trends. If interest rates go up, a larger portion of the payment goes to the interest; if rates go down, more goes to cover the principal.

VA loan. A loan guaranteed by the Department of Veterans Affairs against loss to the lender, and made through a private lender.

ABOUT THE AUTHOR

Mark Rowh is a widely published writer on career topics. His books include *Great Jobs for Political Science Majors*, *Great Jobs for Chemistry Majors*, *Opportunities in Fund-Raising Careers*, *Slam Dunk Cover Letters*, *Winning Government Grants and Contracts for Your Small Business*, and *How to Improve Your Grammar and Usage*.

Rowh has also written for major magazines such as *Consumers Digest*, *The Rotarian*, and *Reader's Digest*, and is a contributing editor for *Office Solutions* magazine.

A graduate of Marshall University and Clemson University, he resides with his family in Virginia.